Reflections of the Civil War in Southern Humor

Also by Wade H. Hall

Conecuh People: Words of Life from the Alabama Black Belt

An Interview with Abraham Lincoln: April 1, 1865

The Outrageous Times of Larry Bruce Mitchell

REFLECTIONS OF THE CIVIL WAR IN SOUTHERN HUMOR

Wade H. Hall

NewSouth Books
Montgomery

NewSouth Books
105 S. Court Street
Montgomery, AL 36104

Library of Congress Cataloging-in-Publication Data

Hall, Wade H.
Reflections of the Civil War in southern humor / Wade H. Hall.
p. cm.

ISBN 978-1-60306-392-0 (paperback)
ISBN 978-1-60306-086-8 (ebook)

1. Confederate States of America—Humor—Social aspects. 2. United States—History—Civil War, 1861-1865—Humor—Social aspects. 3. Wit and humor—Social aspects—Southern States—History—19th century. 4. Southern States—Humor—History—19th century. 5. American wit and humor—Southern States—History and criticism. I. Title.

F214.H35 2011
973.7'130207—dc22

2011016147

Printed in the United States of America

This book was originally published by the University of Florida Press with the LCCN 62063119.

Conquered but not Convinced

Contents

Preface

As one of the organic forms of literature, humor has always responded to and reflected the needs of the people at a given time. A study of a people's humor, I believe, reveals as much about them as an investigation of more somber historical records. And the time spent reading humor is much more enjoyable.

The Civil War and its aftermath were days of the South's greatest need. A less-heroic people would surely have given up fighting for the Cause long before the South did. A less proud people might even have forgotten it by now. Historians have suggested many reasons for the South's fearless stand against "overwhelming numbers and resources," to use General Lee's words. In this short study I merely want to add one reason to the list: the humor of the Southerner—as soldier and civilian—during the war and the bleak days that followed it.

The postwar South was not unlike that mythical bird, the phoenix, which rises reborn from its own ashes. But the South arose from the ashes of humiliation and defeat smiling—though sometimes through tears. The Southerner's sense of humor helped him to fight a war he believed honorable and to accept the bitter defeat which ended it. Without the escape valve of humor, many a "rebel" would have succumbed to despair. The Southerner could smile wistfully as he looked back on a proud past and hopefully as he looked forward to an uncertain future. He smiled because he read humorists like Bill Arp, who once wrote somewhat serio-comically that the South was "conquered but not convinced."

In this study I have attempted to represent all the types of humor written in the South between the beginning of the Civil War and the beginning of World War I, specifically 1861 and 1914, including war memoirs, novels, plays, short stories, poetry, and songs. After a survey of humor written during the war, I discuss the soldier, the Negro, the poor white, and the "folks at home" in wartime, as they are reflected in the postwar humor.

This paper is a revised section of a doctoral dissertation which I completed in September 1961 at the University of Illinois.

For my research I had at my disposal one of the best collections of American humor and folklore in existence, the Franklin J. Meine Collection at the University of Illinois. The Illinois library faculty was extremely accommodating in making the collection accessible to me. Other research included a check of the files of my hometown newspaper, the Union Springs (Alabama) *Herald*, from 1867 to 1914. The specimens of humor I collected from this source gave me a clearer idea of the immense popularity of Civil War humor during the period. I should also like to thank my dissertation adviser, Dr. John T. Flanagan, for his close reading and many helpful suggestions, even though he was three thousand miles away lecturing in Belgium and Germany when he read the manuscript.

Much of the material in this monograph is unknown even to specialists in American history and literature. Most of the resources I used, in fact, are out of print and unavailable generally. I feel, therefore, that the celebration of the Civil War Centennial is a good time to "unearth" this literature from fields that have lain fallow for many years.

Thanks must go to Charles Scribner's Sons for permission to

quote from *War Years with Jeb Stuart* by W. W. Blackford, and to the University of Texas Press for permission to quote from *Rebel Private Front and Rear* by William Andrew Fletcher.

WADE H. HALL

Reflections of the Civil War in Southern Humor

1

During and After the War

The Civil War was not a laughing matter. It was the bloodiest and most bitter war the world had then known. It was the culmination of ill will between the North and the South which had been in the making for decades. It created hatred which took years to dissipate. It killed off the nation's ablest men. It was an American tragedy which could have been avoided. But it was one of the most justifiable wars ever fought, for it showed that the destiny of both North and South must inevitably be one. The business of the war, therefore, was grim and serious because its outcome was to determine the future of "the last best hope of man."

Although a tragedy, this "irrepressible conflict" was not without its lighter side. Comic relief helped lighten the darkness of the tragedy for the people at home and the men at the front. Perhaps paradoxically, the humor associated with the war was less bloody and more refined than the dominant humor of the prewar period, the coarse, painful productions by the so-called humorists of the Old Southwest.

Of all those affected by the war, the Southern soldier was probably without peer in finding humor in it. One observer of the war commented on the humor of the Rebel soldier:

> The Confederate soldier was distinguished for his cheerfulness, and I cannot look back on the scenes around the Confed campfires without amazement at the temper of the men who

> carried the muskets. I wonder how hilarity and sport could animate bivouacs in an atmosphere of discomfort and danger.
>
> Around a campfire, feasting on an ounce of raw pork and cornbread made of unhusked meal, jokes of striking humor and sallies of keen wit always lightened the gloomy hours; on the march every passing person caught shots of ridicule which would almost make a mule laugh; and a line of soldiers on the march, halted for a tardy commissary train, gave occasion for merrymaking and fun as sparkling as rippling water dancing in the sunlight.[1]

Thus the Southern soldier laughed as he fought and died, and his laughter was recorded in chronicle, poetry, fiction, and folklore.

With tempers at the boiling point, it was natural that Civil War humor was intensely bitter and sectional. Few humorists could remain objective and levelheaded. Even the great humorist-conciliator of the postwar period, Joel Chandler Harris, joined as a fledgling writer in the propaganda battle with an unfinished play, *Butler the Beast,* which opened with the Union general Ben Butler saying to an aide: "Well, William, have you sought the city on some pretense or other, to hang a man?"[2] But it was the humor of such partisans as Bill Arp and Petroleum V. Nasby that lightened the burdens of soldiers in the field and of politicians in Richmond and Washington.

Beginning with the election of Lincoln and not abating until Appomattox, the propaganda humorists were busily at work. George Washington Harris's *Sut Lovingood Travels with Old Abe Lincoln* (Chicago, 1937) was an early entry in the field. Published in the Nashville *Union and American* between February 28 and March 5, 1861, this series of sketches tells how the young Tennessee mountaineer helped get Lincoln safely from Springfield to the White House. As an advance scout, Sut uncovers a plot in Baltimore to murder the president, and hurries to Harrisburg, Pennsylvania, to warn him. Replying to Sut's warning, Lincoln admits that he has done "the things I hadn't oughter, and left undone the things I had oughter." He then begs the Tennesseean for advice. Sut comes to the frightened president's aid by disguising him so that "he looked like he'd been on a big drunk for three weeks." According to Sut's account, only his intervention saved the president and got him to Washington to be sworn in. By implication Sut shows that Lincoln is one of his kind: worthless and idiotic. The sketch reveals the dominant Southern attitudes toward the president-elect: he is a coward, intemperate, boorish, ugly. Describing Old Abe, Sut wrote that he looked like "a yeller ladder with half the rungs knocked out." Harris concluded his sketches by comparing Lincoln with a dead frog that had been stretched out of shape. In Washington, Sut gave Lincoln one more bit of advice on how he could get through his term, "Jis take the persishion that you haint sponsibil while onder a skeer an hit will kiver your hole administrashun." During the war the spokesmen for the slavocracy ceased being the well-bred gentlemen of earlier humor and became red-necked louts like Bill Arp, Mozis Addums, and Sut Lovingood. They were all radical secessionists.

The work of Charles H. Smith ("Bill Arp") was to the South what Artemus Ward's was to the North. Written in letter form by a supposedly almost illiterate Georgia cracker, the first Bill Arp sketches were published in a Rome, Georgia, paper, the *Southern Confederacy*. Arp's first letter to Lincoln appeared in April 1861, soon after the taking of Harper's Ferry. It shows the fierce Southern indignation and pride at the beginning of the war and ridicules Lincoln's demand that the Rebels lay down their arms and disperse within twenty days. Arp tells the president sarcastically that it cannot be done in less than thirty days. In his second letter to Lincoln, published in January 1862, Arp laments that "we hav not been able to disperse as yet." After the news of the Emancipation Proclamation reached the South, he published a third letter to the president in December

1862, in which he reported that the South was still buying and selling Negroes. He added, however, that he knows they soon will all be free and will "rush frantikally forth into the arms of their deliverers, and with perfumed and sented gratitude embrace your exsellency, and Madam Harriet Beechers toe." Later in the same month Arp wrote his last letter to Lincoln. He told the president that it was possible "that you are usin too much Proklamation" because over eighteen months before he had ordered "the boys to retire and be peasable" but they had paid him no mind. Now that the president had "proklimated the niggers free," Arp was afraid that this proclamation would also be disregarded. On a more serious note, the Georgia cracker reported that the South was sacrificing willingly in order to whip the North: Southerners "swear by the ghost of Calhoun they will eat roots and drink branch water the balance of the time before they will kernowly to your abolition dyenasty." In the role of adviser to the President, Arp suggested a better route to Richmond than the one the Yankees had been using. Until then, he wrote, the Union army had "been tryin to cum . . . through a mity Longstreet, over two powerful Hills, and across a tremendious Stonewall." He suggested they try going around by the "Rocky Mountings."[3]

Bill Arp, So Called: A Side Show of the Southern Side of the War, published in New York in 1866, contained the four letters to Lincoln and other wartime sketches. Realizing their fiercely partisan nature, Smith explained: "At the time they were written they were appreciated, because the minds of the people needed relaxation from the momentous and absorbing interests of the war" (5).[4] He continued: "For the sentiments that pervade these letters, I have no apology to make. At the time they appeared in the press of the South, these sentiments were the silent echoes of our people's thoughts. . . . Of course they contain exaggerations, and prophecies which were never fulfilled; but both sections were playing 'brag' as well as 'battle,' and though we could not compete with our opponents in the former, yet some of us did try to hold our own. At both games we were whipped by overwhelming forces and we have given it up" (6–7).

The sketches show that Arp was not only critical of the Yankee invaders; he also castigated Southerners for nonsupport or mismanagement of the war. Georgia's Governor Joseph Brown was a favorite target. One time Arp wrote: "Durn old Brown. He is as big a fool on a proclamation as old Abe Lincoln" (41). Indicting Brown's alleged autocracy: "Joe Brown orders me to jail; I appeal to a special jury and Joe Brown is the jury. I carry it to the Supreme Court, and Joe Brown is the court. . . . Brown's got us, and I reckon it's the best plan to humor the joke. . . . 'Three cheers for Joe Brown,' that's the way to say it" (50–51). Accusing Brown of presidential ambitions, Arp wrote: "Sometimes I think you are trying to climb too fast, Joe. You see your ideas get so much elevation that your head gets dizzy and your brain begins to swim, and you naturally overlook some things and commit indiscretions which are distressing" (62). He once accused Brown of having the same motto as Louis XIV, "L'Etat? C'est moi."

Draft dodgers and shirkers also came in for criticism from Arp's acid pen. In a sketch on extortioners he wrote: "It seems utterly impossible to get the extortioners in the ranks. Governor Brown thought he would put some of 'em to the useful art of bullet-stopping, so he called for a draft. Enough of the patriotic responded, and there was no draft. But it give 'em a powerful scare, and developed more rheumatics and chronics than was thought possible to exist in a limestone country" (31). The flower of Southern manhood, he feared, was being killed: "We will have a race of people after a while that ain't worth a curse. The good ones are getting killed up, but these *skulkers* and *shirkers* and *dodgers* don't die" (46). He wrote sarcastically another time: "Such is the rapid progress of human events in these fighting times, that a man who was only forty last year, can be forty-six this year." If he were a doctor, he adds, "I would cure 'em or kill 'em, and then our poor, bleeding country would have sound men or none; and that's the way to stop dodging around" (78–79).

That the South was never unanimously behind the Confederacy is made clear throughout Arp's sketches. Forgetting that war calls for curtailment of many rights of citizenship, Arp and others excoriated Confederate politicians for the secret legislative session—"perhaps a little the closest communion ever established in a well-watered country"—and the suspension of habeas corpus—"perhaps, when suspended, the most savagerous beast that ever got after tories and traders." In "A Message to All Folks" he summarized major grievances against the Confederate government: "F-E-L-L-E-R CITIZENS: The war, and the Yankees, and old Lincoln and his threats of subjugation, extermination, amalgamation, desolation, and Mr. Toombs' foul domination, is a big thing, terrible and horrible. But old Habeas *hung up*, and secret sessions, and the currency bill, and conscription are far bigger, and awful in the extreme. Our soldiers ought to let the Yankees alone, and come home and fight these savage beasts, and you, my fellow-citizens, ought to arm yourselves with sticks, and rocks, and thrashpoles, and hot water, and pikes, and make a violent assault upon these 'most monstrous paradoxes'" (55). Even the generals tasted his venom. "Since the discovery of America by Pocahontas, the habeas corpus has never been suspended over anybody, except three hundred thousand soldiers in the Confederate army. For nearly three years, General Lee and Johnston have had it suspended over all the fighting boys in their commands" (58–59).

The main object of Arp's war satire was, naturally, the North and especially its conduct of the war. Arp's epithets for the Yankee soldier included "foul invader," "miscegenator," and "blue devil."

Northern versions of what the Federal armies were doing were usually exaggerated, he maintained, and in several sketches he attempted to set the record straight. About the Yankee raid, or "battle," in Rome, he commented: "I think it highly proper you should git the strait of it from one who seen it with his eyes, and heard it with his years, and a piece of it fell on his big toe" (35). Although fighting against overwhelming odds, the Southern defenders were heroic. "For three days and nights our valiant troops had beat back the foul invader, and saved our pullets from their devouring jaws" (85). But eventually the city had to be evacuated and left to the Yankees. Only a few renegade Negroes remained behind to welcome the enemy: "It is a source of regret, however, that some of our households of the African scent have fallen back into the arms of the foul invaders. I suppose they may now be called miscegenators, and by this time are increasing the stock of Odour d'Afrique in Northern society, which popular perfume crowds out of the market all those extracts which made X. Bazin, Jules Haule and Lubin famous. Good-bye, sweet otto of roses; farewell, ye balm of a thousand flowers—your days are numbered" (91). The conduct of the Yankee soldiers in Rome, he reported, was despicable. The "heartless, pitiless invaders" even used tombstones like rocks in building fortifications.

When the war tide was obviously going against the South, Arp could still see some hope for success. Of the mounted Rebel soldier, for instance, he wrote: "The truth is, that the Confederate cavalry can fight 'em, and dog 'em, and dodge 'em, and bushwhack 'em, and bedevil 'em, for a thousand years. . . ." The Rebel cavalry, he maintained, was invincible (118).

In several sketches Arp was realistic about the chances for a Southern victory. Usually, though, in speculating on a Northern victory he became defiant. Near the end of the war he wrote of Lincoln: "After he has whipped us, then he has got to subjugate us." This, the rabid Rebel asserted, could not be done. All the hullabaloo about Lincoln's freeing of the slave was nonsense, he continued; and, foreshadowing the tone of his immediate postwar pieces, he wrote: "What does it all amount to?—I want to buy a nigger, and I had just as lief buy a chunk of a free nigger as any other sort. I don't care a bobee about his being free, if I can subjugate him; and if he gets above his color, I will put thirty-nine whelks right under his shirt, and make him wish that old Lincoln stood in his shoes" (115). With these words Arp set the stage for the conflict of Reconstruction.

Southern humor written during the war was by no means restricted to prose. Comic songs and poems were also popular. One of the most popular rebel songs was "Eating Goober Peas," which contained such verses as:

Just before the battle the Gen'ral hears a row.
He says, "The Yanks are coming, I hear their rifles now"
He turns around in wonder, and what do you think he sees?
The Georgia Militia, eating goober peas![5]

A couplet expressed a longing for the end of the war in these words: *"I wish this war was over, when free from rags and fleas, / We'd kiss our wives and sweethearts, and gobble goober peas!"*

One of the most widely reprinted poetic satires in the wartime South was the "Confederate Mother Goose," written in the Richmond office of Dr. George W. Bagby's *Southern Literary Messenger* by Bagby, Innes Randolph, William M. Burwell, Will Washington, and others who made up the group known as the Richmond Wits. Seizing upon well-known weaknesses or shortcomings of Union generals, the wits came up with such gems as the following:

Little Be-Pope, he lost his hope,
Jackson, the Rebel, to find him;

But he found him at last, and he ran very fast,
With his bully invaders behind him!
Little McClellan sat eating a mellon,
The Chickahominy by.
He stuck in a spade; and a long time delayed,
Then cried: "What a great general am I!"
Hey! diddle Sutler, the dastard Ben Butler,
Fought women, morn, evening and noon;
And old Satan laughed, as hot brimstone he quaffed,
When the Beast ran away with the Spoon![6]

Most Southern war humor naturally showed up the foibles of the North. President Lincoln was the most popular target of Southern wit, with the cautious General McClellan a close second. A parody of Hamlet's soliloquy is "McClellan's Soliloquy," by "a Daughter of Georgia." The poem pillories the wavering general who, Lincoln complained, had "the slows."

Advance, or not advance; that is the question!
Whether 'tis better in the mind to suffer
The jeers and howlings of outrageous Congressmen,
Or to take arms against a host of rebels,
And, by opposing, beat them?—To fight—to win—
No more; and by a victory, to say we end
This war, and all the thousand dreadful shocks
The flesh's exposed to—'tis a consummation
Devoutly to be wished. To fight, to win,
To beat! perchance be beaten;—ay, there's the rub;
After a great defeat, what would ensue!
When we have shuffled off the battle-field,
Must give us pause; there's the respect
That makes calamity a great defeat.

But shall I bear the scorn of all the North,
The "outward" pressure, and Old Abe's reviling,
The pangs of being scoffed at for this long delay,
The turning out of office (ay, perchance,
When I myself might now my greatness make
With a great battle)? I'd not longer bear
To drill and practice troops behind intrenchments,
But that the fear of meeting with the foe
On dread Manassas, from whose plains
Few of us would return—puzzles my will,
And makes me rather bear the evils I have,
Than fly to others which are greater far.
These Southerners make cowards of us all.[7]

Southern optimism and pride dominate the parody. After the war only the pride remained.

The popularity after the war of humorous accounts and anecdotes of the war is perhaps astounding in this more sober mid-twentieth-century. It must be remembered, however, that this was a country, split though it was, which made heroes of its humorists—a nation whose slain president had been its most prominent humorist. The times were serious, but the ultimate aim of much of the humor was also serious. A joke, some sage once remarked, is the most solemn thing in the world. Hence the increased popularity of humor among post-Civil War Americans was no indictment of their lack of seriousness; it was rather a testimony of their concern for it.

The most popular means of disseminating humor in the post-war South was the newspaper. For many years following the war, newspapers were filled with war humor. The following anecdote taken from a rural weekly soon after the end of hostilities is typical:

> We have read many amusing specimens of soldier wit during

> the late war; but as good as we have seen was the reply of a Virginia cavalryman to a North Carolina infantryman. It was on the march toward Adairsville, in November, 1863, a cold, bright morning, while the troops were lying along the road waiting for obstacles to be removed in front. A fellow came jogging down the line on an old flea-bitten frame of a horse, and as he passed a chap greeted him with—"I say, mister, you are mighty like a brother of mine the hogs eat up." The cavalryman did not relax a muscle, but looking the "tar heel" straight in the face, replied: "Well, my friend, 'tis a monstrous pity they hadn't finished the family while they *war a eatin'*," and moved on amidst shouts of laughter.[8]

The Sunny South, published in Atlanta, ca. 1894, carried a regular column called "The Gray and the Blue" which contained minutiae of the war, including many humorous selections. Southern magazines which featured the humor of the camp included *Scott's Monthly Magazine* of Atlanta (1865–69) and the *Southern Bivouac* of Louisville (1882–87). The quality of such popular humor was not always high, but it filled empty columns and the readers liked it.

Postwar collections of campaign humor became best sellers. Usually the anthologies contained humor representing both the blue and the gray. Occasionally some bitterness and bias is evident in the selections, but most were good-natured and contributed to a better understanding between conqueror and conquered. Through the catharsis of laughter, much ill will was purged away.[9]

Many of the ablest writers in the South dealt with the humor of the war. Indeed for some the war provided the inspiration for their best work. In an essay published in 1907 Charles W. Kent concluded that Thomas Nelson Page's "best short stories are those that record in true Hanover negro dialect war time in Old Virginia."[10] Other humorists from Maryland to Texas spilled much ink in relating or creating the humors of the late war.

In addition to their obvious motive of entertainment, the humorists contributed to a fuller understanding and an objective interpretation of the war. Some even made significant contributions to the development of realism in American literature. One critic placed them in the vanguard of realistic treatments of the war: "The first and the most consistently realistic attitude toward the war in the literature before 1870 is to be found in the fiction created by the popular humorists. . . . Charles H. Smith's Bill Arp, the spokesman of commonsense in the Confederacy, is not unlike Artemus Ward in his blunt, kindly views. Arp, Mrs. Arp, the children, Tip, Potash, and all the 'runagees' and slackers of middle Georgia mingle together in a scene that is not romantic. The humorists deliberately set out to tell the truth."[11] Although Smith's realistic comments on the war date chiefly before April 1865, he continued his bitter denunciation of black Republicans and turncoat Rebels through his rustic mouthpiece Bill Arp into the 1870s.

The war furnished an inexhaustible supply of incidents for humorists to use in their imagery. The humorist for the *Atlanta Constitution*, Sam W. Small, for example, had his Negro creation, Old Si, describe a grasshopper plague on his two-acre homestead in this manner: "An' yer nebber seed sech forrigin' an' instrueshun ob truck in de feel's sence de days when de Linkum army cum 'long hyar!"[12] So the fact and folklore of the war were assimilated into the stock of humorous metaphor. From Joel Chandler Harris to William Faulkner, Southern writers have drawn freely from this reservoir.

Notes

1. Colonel William H. Stewart, *The Spirit of the South* (New York, 1908), 107.
2. Julia Collier Harris, *The Life and Letters of Joel Chandler Harris* (Boston, 1918), 46.
3. For a good estimate of Smith's early work, including these letters, see Jeannette Tandy, *Crackerbox Philosophers in American Humor and Satire* (New

York, 1925), chap. 5.

4. Numbers in parentheses at the ends of quotations represent page numbers in the volume referred to.
5. Quoted in B. A. Botkin (ed.), *A Treasury of Southern Folklore* (New York, 1949), 716.
6. Quoted in T. C. DeLeon, *Belles, Beaux and Brains of the 60's* (New York, 1907), 268–70.
7. Frank Moore (ed.), *Anecdotes, Poetry and Incidents of the War* (Boston, 1866), 358.
8. Union Springs (Ala.) *Times*, Dec. 7, 1867, 4.
9. The popularity of the Civil War as a subject for humor did not wane in the twentieth century; an anthology edited by Katharine M. Jones, *New Confederate Short Stories* (Columbia, S.C., 1954), contains humor by such writers as Caroline Gordon, O. Henry, James Street, and Frances Gray Patton.
10. *Library of Southern Literature*, IX, 3851.
11. Rebecca Washington, "The Civil War and Its Aftermath in American Fiction, 1861–1899" (unpublished dissertation, University of Chicago, 1937), 11.
12. *Old Si's Sayings* (Chicago, 1886), 115.

2

The Soldiers

The most popular postwar subject of Civil War humor was logically the soldier. His war experiences were exploited in poetry, fiction, memoirs, and anecdotes. The humor dealt with soldiers of all ranks, from privates to generals. Even soldiers from European countries, in the South as observers, were the subject of humorous sketches. Not even the Yankee soldier was excepted.

Most of the humor concerning the Yankee soldier was satirical. Using satire, the Southern humorist gave vent to feelings of hurt and wrong he felt the South had suffered at the hands of the Northern soldiers. There was no more vulnerable target for the South's satire than General Ben Butler, known popularly below the Potomac as "Beast" Butler, the Union general who gained fame—or infamy—as military commander of New Orleans after its fall. *The American Cyclops*, a poem by J. Fairfax McLaughlin, published in Baltimore in 1868 under the pseudonym "Pasquino," impaled Butler with the poinards of heroic couplets. A passage from the poem will illustrate the "Beast's" popularity in Dixie:

Oh! hapless hour, when from the stormy North,
This modern Cyclops marched repellent forth,
To slake his thirst for blood and plundered wealth,
Not as the soldier, but by fraud and stealth;
To waft the gales of death with horror rife
On helpless age, and wage with women strife:

To leave Baltimore and New Orleans
The drunkard's name, or worse, the gibbet's scenes;
To license lust with all a lecher's rage,
And stab the virtue of a Christian age:
This single crime will fix a beastly name,
Fresh in immortal infamy and shame.

For many years the name Butler, along with Grant and Sherman, conjured repulsion in the Southern mind and rebellion in the Southern heart. The Southern humorist capitalized on the despised Yankee generals' public images and caricatured them even more.

An anonymous poem parodying the contemporary poet-laureate Tennyson's "Come Not When I Am Dead" was probably written, the paragrapher for the Union Springs *Times* (September 4, 1867) noted, by a soldier who had been present at the siege of Vicksburg:

Come not when I'm asleep,
To rain huge fragments on my lowly head,
To cause with fear my tingling veins to creep,
Or add me to the patriotic dead!
There let the Minnies fall and Parrots fly—
But thou—pass by!
Shell! whether aimed by accident,
I care not, nor appreciate thee just;
Strike where thou wilt, but I am sick of shot,
And I desire to rest,
Pass on, oh shell, and leave me where I lie,
Go by—go by!

Whether written during or shortly after the war, the humor of the parody is of the nervous kind found in the works of authors "who were there" and can see danger in a retrospect of mixed humor and fear.

Fictional humor by postwar Southern writers dealing with soldier life includes sketches by Will Harben, Charles H. Smith, Sidney Lanier, George Washington Cable, and Joel Chandler Harris.

Will Harben's *Northern Georgia Sketches* (Chicago, 1902) includes one story set during the War Between the States. Like many postwar humorous stories, "The Courage of Ericson" shows how the opposing sides of the war could be reconciled (229–51). It is the story of the estrangement of a Rebel boy and his Union-sympathizing girl and their subsequent reconciliation as a result of his being wounded in a battle near the girl's house. When the boy first shows up at the girl's house, she affects to despise him because of the uniform he has on; but when she sees that he is wounded and hears that the Yanks are out looking for escaped Rebels, she tries to save him by getting him to dress in her dead brother's Federal uniform. He patriotically refuses, but faints in time for the girl and her father to dress him in the Yankee uniform before the search party arrives.

The girl tells the Yankee captain who comes in that the boy's mind has been affected by his wound and that he is irrational. Should he come to, she tells the Union officer, he might even say he's a Reb. She explains: "Once he declared to us that he was actu'ly President Jeff Davis. Thar's no tellin' what idea may strike 'im next." Sure enough, when the Rebel regains consciousness and sees the hated uniform of the enemy on him, he shouts belligerently: "Why, who's done this heer? . . . I ain't no Yankee soldier. I'm a rebel dyed in the wool." He is unable to convince the search party, however, and when they leave he mutters: "I didn't 'low you'd play sech a dog-mean trick on me, Sally. . . . I'd ruther a thousand times 'a' been shot like a soldier than to hide in Yankee clothes." While he is convalescing at his girl's house, his partisan fervor gradually subsides; and when the news of Lee's surrender comes he can say: "I'm awfully glad it's all over. . . . I'm satisfied. I was shot by a Yankee ball an' nussed back to life by a Union gal, so I reckon my account is even" (247–51). Like the stronger union of states forged by the fiery war, so two young people are ultimately reunited by the pressures of opposing sympathies. They are brought together by a Georgia local colorist.

Sidney Lanier was a child of his time in using excessive sentiment. To relieve the heavy sentimentality of his war novel, *Tiger-Lilies*, Lanier occasionally employed grotesque humor. According to Aubrey Harrison Starke, the novel reveals a mixture of "the serious and the comic, the sublime and the grotesque, the pathetic and the ludicrous."[1] Much of the humorous material for the novel comes from Lanier's own war experiences. One such experience concerned his unfortunate hesitation to "borrow" a clean new shirt off the corpse of a Union private: "He hesitated for a moment, but quickly deciding that he could not take the shirt, moved on. Within a few minutes he had repented his squeamishness, reminding himself of his sore need of a whole garment, and urging upon himself the strong probability that the Federal would not, under the circumstances, begrudge the transfer. By the time he had returned, however, he found to his chagrin that a less tender conscienced mate had dexterously captured the shirt."[2]

Lanier's kinship with the earlier backwoods humor is made explicit in *Tiger-Lilies*, not only in its grotesquerie, but in its treatment of pain. Starke wrote: "Lanier's sense of humor was seldom subtle: he liked puns, and minor physical discomfiture amused him tremendously; the most amusing part of the description of the ball in Chapter XII is ridiculous to the point of utter improbability. Ruebetsahl as King Arthur and Cranston as Lancelot fight a duel which almost ends in the death of Cranston but the spectators think it only a part of the masquerade" (96). Throughout the novel Lanier demonstrated that his humor retained vestiges of the older coarse school of George W. Harris and Johnson J. Hooper. A veteran of the war, he surely had material for realistic sketches that would have shocked the sensibilities of his readers; but he bowed to convention.

Although remembered primarily for his local-color sketches of the Louisiana Creoles, George Washington Cable also treated the Civil War soldier in his fiction. The novels *Dr. Sevier* and *The Cavalier* contain war humor. *The Cavalier* (New York, 1901), at least partly autobiographical, is the record of the war experiences of a nineteen-year-old "cavalier," Richard Smith of New Orleans. Richard was a member of a scout unit and his work was extremely dangerous; however, the tension was relieved by many touches of humor, much of it played on him. Because of his youth he was often the butt of harmless practical jokes pulled by the older, more experienced soldiers. Cable exploited the cavalier's innocence and immaturity. The character's reactions to trying or unusual situations, for example, are often amusing. One day he singlehandedly captured a Yankee soldier. Speaking in the first person, the boy related the scene:

> "I surrender," he said, with amiable ease. I stepped back a pace and he drew out and straightened up—the tallest man I had ever seen. I laughed, he smiled, laughed; my eyes filled with tears, I blazed with rage, and in plain sight and hearing of those ladies [refugee ladies the boy is escorting to safety] he said, "That's all right, my son, get as scared as you like; only, you don't need to cry about it."
>
> "Hold your tongue!" I barked my wrath like a frightened puppy, drawing back a stride and laying my eye closer along the pistol. "If you call me your son again I'll send you to your fathers" (39–40).

Having the cavalier tell his own story in his own words makes the "education" of the young recruit in the ways of war even more touching.

The creator of Uncle Remus also dealt often in his fiction with the Civil War soldier. Like most of his works, Joel Chandler Harris's war stories were written to show both North and South that the adversaries had been people who were kind and honorable and had fought for what they thought was right. Although a Georgian, Harris presented in all of his war fiction a very sympathetic picture of the North. The heroine of the novel *A Little Union Scout* is, in fact, a Federal spy. Most of the stories in *Tales of the Home Folks* ignore the grimmer aspects of the war on both sides.

In *The Shadow Between His Shoulder-Blades* (Boston, 1907) Harris used as a narrator his humorous Georgia cracker Billy Sanders. Most of the humor in the novel derives from the manner in which Billy tells his adventures. Sitting on the tavern veranda in Shady Dale and surrounded by curious auditors, Billy tells in cracker dialect of the part he played as a soldier in the conflict. He had acted as a nineteenth-century Sancho to a local aristocrat, Wimberly Driscoll, who had returned home wounded but before long was "sufferin' from the corns on the foot he left in Virginia." Thirsting for battle glory, the two decide to set out in search of General Forrest's outfit. As they are leaving, Driscoll's Negro mammy puts up a big howl, and Sanders comments for the benefit of his Yankee listeners, "Ef one of you Northern fellers could 'a' heern 'er, you'd 'a' got a bran' new idee in regards to the oppressed colored people" (12). Most of the novel is concerned with the entertaining but dangerous adventures of the aristocrat and the cracker during the war. As a reconciliationist, Harris never allows Billy Sanders to express anything reproachful against the Yankees; on the contrary, Billy's harshest criticism concerns a Southern opportunist.

Well into the twentieth century the favorite pastime of Civil War survivors, it seems, was the writing of war memoirs, many with a humorous slant. These memoirs provide intimate glimpses of soldier life by men who were soldiers themselves. As the war receded into the past, their recollections became extremely conciliatory, with little or no criticism of the North. They were written by privates and generals and all the ranks in between. Most purport to tell what actually happened, although many professional writers used their war experiences as a springboard for the imagination. Joel Chandler Harris, for example, combined fact and fiction in *On the Plantation.* George Washington Cable served briefly in the Confederate cavalry and probably used his experiences as the basis for his story of a raw young recruit in *The Cavalier.* Neither Harris nor Cable was ever a violently partisan Rebel, and in the reflective aftermath of the war each saw the absurdity of the conflict.

There was probably not an officer on either side who did not at least plan to write his memoirs of the important part he played in the war. And if he happened to die before accomplishing this mission, usually an obliging kinsman would immortalize his deeds on paper. Frank A. Montgomery performed this service in *Reminiscences of a Mississippian in Peace and War* (Cincinnati, 1901) for his relative, Major W. E. Montgomery, whose command was called featherbeds "because they always scattered at night and slept in their own or other people's houses" (116). The memoirs include many amusing incidents—such as how the major once escaped his Union captors. After he was captured, the major was taken to a house surrounded by cane. Pretending that something was wrong with him, he asked his guard to walk around the yard with him. While they were promenading around the house, the guard asked him about the game in that part of the country, and the major replied that there were plenty of bears. Just then a noise was made in the cane by a cow or mule, and the Rebel, seeing his chance, shouted, "There's one now," and taking his captor off guard he made his escape into the cane. Surely many an unreconstructed Southerner delighted to read of such clever escapes which made the unsuspecting Yanks look foolish and inferior.

Most memoirs were written with a twofold purpose: to entertain and to inform. In the preface to *War Years with Jeb Stuart* (New York, 1945) Lieutenant Colonel W. W. Blackford, C.S.A., wrote that he hoped his sketches would be useful to the historian and entertaining to the general reader. He achieved his entertainment motif with touches of humor scattered throughout the book. He recalled that once when he was captured by his own men at night they wouldn't believe that he had on a Confederate uniform until he allowed them to feel of the lace on his sleeve.

Humorous incidents such as the following, after the surrender at Harper's Ferry, relieve the pathos and gruesomeness:

> The men of the surrendered garrison, not having been exposed to the weather, were not all sunburned, and this paleness to us at the time looked peculiar in soldiers, contrasting so strongly with our berry-brown complexions. As we marched along the street one of our troopers sang out to one of the men on the sidewalk, "I say, Yank, what sort of soap do you fellows use? It has washed all the color out of your faces," at which our side cheered. To this the man retorted, "Damn me, if you don't look like you had never used soap of any sort." Shouts of laughter greeted the reply from our men as well as the Yanks, and our man called back as he rode on, "Bully for you, Yank; you got me that time" (146).

If Blackford is to be believed, all was not animosity between Rebs and Yanks. Although they fought each other when commanded to, humor was a common ground on which both sides could meet without guns and sabers.

But relations between the blues and grays could be bitter. Humor could be grim, and fun might become tragedy:

> Rather a curious incident happened one day between the infantry lines, which at that place were about three hundred yards apart. About midway there was a farm house and around it wandered a solitary turkey which a Yankee skirmisher shot and then ran forward to secure amid cheers from his side; as he stooped to pick up the turkey one of our men shot him dead and ran forward to get the prize amid cheers from our side. Just as he stooped to pull the turkey from under the Yankee, a shot from their side killed him and wild cheers from their side arose; and there they all three lay one on top of the other, neither side wanting turkey any more (243–44).

Blackford offers an explanation for the tragic incident by adding: "Men in the infantry have such a hard time of it and see so little fun that when a chance offers they are just like children." But the toys of soldiers are loaded guns.

A simple event could be occasion for the greatest merriment. Blackford remembered, for instance, the time when a cat broke the tension of waiting for a Yankee attack:

> Just then a young Lieutenant sitting at the end of the table . . . got so nervous that he slipped under the table; this started a titter among the others, which an instant later burst into an irrepressible roar of laughter from a most unexpected event. As I have said, the common above the fly was a resort for cats from the town at night, and these cats, hearing the fearful noise above them, and seeing the long stream of fire shooting towards them from the heavens, became completely demoralized and went scampering by as fast as they could run, back to the deserted houses where they made their home. One huge tomcat, however, came tearing down the hill with eyes flaming, claws out, and hair on end, directly towards my fly. He was going so fast that he could not

> avoid the pit in which the fly stood, but came dashing, spitting and sputtering with one bound flop on the table, and with another clear out at the front and away (273–74).

The entire group was convulsed with laughter. The appearance of the cat relieved everyone, including the young lieutenant under the table. Not only did such incidents do much to sustain the soldier; after the war had been lost the defeated South could read of them and in the resultant laughter could gain strength for the future.

Blackford gave many glimpses of the unheroic side of military life, from the stealing of corn for the horses to objective accounts of the slaughtering of men in battle. Though his record is often frank, it contains little or no malice toward the former enemy. He prefers to write about how he and his men were forced to meet the demands of the war in foraging food. Like almost every Confederate unit, they were frequently hungry; hearing a cowbell one day he sent out a detail to capture a small heifer. Unwilling to wait for the meat to be cooked, they ate it raw; and Blackford remembered: "I was surprised to find how good it was. Indeed I could discover no difference between this and rare beef steak, it was so warm and nice" (286).

George Cary Eggleston, the brother of the author of *The Hoosier Schoolmaster*, feeling a bond of sympathy to his Virginia forebears, served as an officer in the Southern army. In 1874, at the request of William Dean Howells, he published *A Rebel's Recollections*, "my reminiscences of life as a Southern soldier." When Howells first approached him to write his memoirs—he says in the preface to the fourth edition—he hesitated, because "at that time war passions had only just begun to cool"; but deciding that he could do something to bring about better feeling between the North and the South, he relented.

Eggleston's personal record of the war contains many humorous sidelights, from comments on Southern female patriotism to inflation in the Confederacy. The intensity of feeling by Southern women is illustrated by a conversation he says he overheard between two ladies. The first said: "I'm sure I do not hate our enemies. I earnestly hope their souls may go to heaven, but I would like to blow all their mortal bodies away, as fast as they come upon our soil." The second lady replied quickly: "Why, you shock me, my dear; I don't see why you want the Yankees to go to heaven! I hope to get there myself some day, and I'm sure I shouldn't want to go if I thought I should find any of them there" (61). The Hoosier Rebel again tells of several ladies living near where a battle was about to commence. They rushed from their house to ask General Forrest what they could do to help. Eggleston recorded that the general told them: "I really don't see that you can do much, except to stand on stumps, wave your bonnets, and shout 'Hurrah, boys!'" (66).

Inflation was always a problem in the Confederacy; but when the South seemed certain to lose the war, it became acute. Eggleston condensed the problem into anecdotal form by relating the conversation between a Union picket and a Confederate picket. The Federal asks if times are hard with coffee $40 a pound, but the Rebel answers truthfully: "Well, perhaps it is a trifle uppish, but then you never saw money so plentiful as it is with us. We hardly know what to do with it, and don't mind paying high prices for things we want" (81).

F. E. Daniel in his *Recollections of a Rebel Surgeon* (Chicago, 1901) also has something to say about Confederate inflation: "I remember one day I bought a wagon-load of home-tanned leather from a countryman, and without unloading it from the wagon, sold it to the town storekeeper at $1200 profit; and made $2000 on a barrel of peach brandy after drinking off of it a week." Daniel's spokesman, "the old Doctor," reminisces about many other things, too. Most of his memories are humorous, some are sad and pathetic, but all are based on fact. He says that the incidents related in his memoirs have little to do with the professional duties of the army surgeon "but are for the most part recollections of fun, frolic, fishing or flirting, as the case may be, 'endurin' of the war,' in the doctor's 'sappy' days" (7–8). Although disapproving of slavery and secession, the Old Doctor had cast his lot with his native Mississippi when she left the Union.

Early in his recollections the doctor articulated the way he and most of the postwar South wanted to look at the war—through rose-colored glasses. Once when talking about the blot of slavery, he stopped and explained to his imaginary auditor: "But look here, Dan'els, I don't like to talk about unpleasant things; it's against my principles, and it's against the principles of my Retroscope" (12–13). His Retroscope, he reminded himself, was like a telescope in that it brought the past closer; but it was unusual in that it brought out "conspicuously and in bold relief, all the pleasant things, all the funny things, all the amusing or ridiculous memories, and of suppressing or effacing the painful, disagreeable ones, or rounding off the rough edges, at least." He then summed up his retroscopic creed: "It's a fact. When we look back at the war, with all its horrors and sufferings, it is remarkable that my memory brings to light mainly the funny side, or the pleasant side, of those days of privations and sacrifice and suffering" (13). Throughout the book, when he was on the verge of describing the war realistically, he remembered his Retroscope and changed his tone. For example, he began to describe the scene after a cavalry charge. "I went up with the ambulances. Oh, horrors upon horrors. Who can depict the horrors of a battlefield after such butchery. Shame upon shame! Brother, of one blood, of one race! Let's drop the curtain. It makes me sick even now to think of what I saw that night, and the next, and the next." And then he broke off. "I wouldn't, if I could, describe it. My Retroscope goes back on me, and I am glad of it; don't know how I ever got onto such a disagreeable subject, unless it was that bad cigar I smoked awhile ago" (82–83).

The first sketch, which the Old Doctor entitled "Sunshine Soldiering," deals with his first days as a soldier, when, he says, "We just ate, and flirted, and drilled, and *played* soldier." When his company was shipped from Jackson to Corinth, he took with him a valise containing broadcloth shirts, patent leather shoes, linen shirts, and fancy socks and ties; but all this was left behind when an order came down that all clothing would be carried on the back. He remembered that "instead of fine clothes we were reduced to a coarse gray flannel shirt, blue cotton pants and a belt." Thus began the dispelling of his romantic notions about war. Life as a whole in the army remained pleasant, until his company started on a forced march: "On our first march I found my knapsack too heavy, and I went through it to lighten it. I took out my extra drawers, my extra undershirts, my extra socks (we wore a flannel topshirt all the while; didn't *need* change) I couldn't throw any of them away; my towel and soap, couldn't spare them; my smoking-tobacco—couldn't find a blessed thing that I could throw away, except two sheets of letter-paper and two envelopes, on which I had expected to write to my sweetheart; fact!" (20–21). Nevertheless, his Retroscope had little trouble showing the light side of army life.

The humor of "The Doctor Gets Dinner" (25–29) is as close as the Old Doctor ever came to the painful humor of before the war. This sketch concerns the time the company cook got sick and the men had to take turns cooking. Knowing very little about cooking—but keeping his ignorance a secret—the Old Doctor, "a little pale-faced, beardless, dandified medical student," decided to cook all the rations he received from the commissary at one time. George, one of his messmates, told him to cook about a peck of rice; so he filled the four-gallon camp-kettle half full of rice, finished filling it with water, and set it on a hot fire. "Presently it began to boil, and, oh, horrors! to slop over." George suggested that he put the excess in the eating vessels; so he filled the coffeepot, and all the tin cups, plates, and pans—but the rice in the kettle kept expanding. Looking around for something more to hold the huge surplus, they saw their friend Bright's big horse-leather boots. George suggested they put rice in them, assuring the doctor that it would cool before Bright could awaken and put his feet into them. They both agreed that this would be a good joke and filled Bright's boots with steaming rice. Unfortunately for their joke, at that moment the captain called to Bright that a lady was there to see him. The Old Doctor recalled the scene in these words: "Bright sat up, rubbing his eyes; and as quick as he could, seized one boot, and socked his foot into the scalding rice; when, gee-whiz! what a howl went up, of mingled pain, wrath and surprise! He made the atmosphere thick with a most florid rhetoric; and with his scalded foot still smoking, and redolent of rice, lit out after me and George with a six-shooter in each hand" (29). Although the physical pain is central here and provides most of the humor, the sketch does not suggest the sadistic Sut Lovingood school. The humor derives rather from the unexpected happening.

Like most war memoirs, Daniel's recollections offer dramatic interpretations of soldier life not found in more somber history. The destruction of food when retreating is an example. The doctor lamented the necessity of destroying food when there were thousands of men hungry; however, he managed to salvage some of it by handing it out to passing infantrymen. He recalled the serio-comic scene in these words: "Well, sirs, it was the funniest sight you ever saw (however, as you didn't see it we'll say the funniest sight imaginable), to see about six miles of bayonets, each one bearing aloft a side of bacon, or a ham, or a bolt of jeans! The hot sun made the grease run out of the meat in streams, and it trickled down on the fellers' faces, and necks, and backs, and then the red dust would settle on it, and it was a funny combination; they looked like a bedraggled *Mardi Gras*" (92). Such descriptions have to be taken from real life. They are too ludicrous for fiction.

Mixed in with Daniel's humorous recollections of the war are many pathetic scenes. He remembered, for example, a dead boy who still clutched an ambrotype in his cold hands: "We took it tenderly from his grasp; it was the picture of a plain, faded, wrinkled old woman of the commoner sort, the poorer country people. It was his *mother.* Ah, to his childish eyes she was not old, nor wrinkled, nor ugly, nor faded, nor common. To him she was beautiful; she was young; she was the apotheosis of all that was lovely and lovable" (95). Daniel did not apologize for this tearful picture. To him and to most of his contemporaries, pathos and humor were but the two sides of the same coin.

The horrors of the war that offer no such cathartic cleansing by tears frequently intrude; but remembering his principles the Old Doctor dispelled them. One day he explained to his biographer why he was in bad humor: "I've been lookin' thro' the wrong end of my Retroscope, contrary to my principles, and before I was aware of it, there had come trooping before my mental vision a whole lot of unpleasant recollections, and it has depressed me somewhat, and I haven't gotten entirely over it, altho' I have taken a bath and disinfected myself" (97). Disinfecting himself with a mixture of James Whitcomb Riley and Mark Twain, he vowed to think only of pleasant things. However, the nightmares of the past continued to rise occasionally in his memory.

Daniel used an emphasis on trivial incidents as an effective way of keeping down bad memories. For instance, he recalled a mock-serious report he submitted to the medical director of the hospital where he was a staff doctor. When the director indicated that medical officers should show more zeal in their work by submitting more detailed reports than the usual four lines saying perfunctorily that everything was satisfactory, the young doctor decided to have a little fun with the language. He wrote a report of twenty-four pages which said no more than the earlier four-line reports. He prefaced his verbiage with:

> The English language is happily so constructed that a great many words of diverse origin and derivation can be so brought to bear as to convey one and the same idea; and consequently, one best versed in the resources of the language will naturally be most facile in its use. Thus, I said, to give an illustration: Instead of saying as Dr. Brown did yesterday, that the bread was a little scorched, it might be expressed thus:
>
> In consequence of inattention, ignorance, incompetence, temporary absence or preoccupation of the colored divinity who presides over the culinary establishment of Ward 3, vulgarly called the "cook," a part of the nutriment, the subsistence, the "grub," a very essential part, which was that day being prepared and intended for the alimentation and sustenance of the unfortunate beings who, by accident, exposure or fate were at that time sick or wounded, and lying prone on a roughly extemporized bunk in a building near by, by courtesy called a hospital, sick, wounded or else convalescent, and dependent on others, ourselves, to-wit, and deprived, doubtless much to their sorrow and regret, of the privilege of being at the front in the trenches or on the lines of battle, battling for their country; to-wit, the bread, being too long exposed to the oxidizing influence of the oven, has been somewhat scorched, burnt, or otherwise injured, being thereby rendered unwholesome and unfit for the purposes for which it was intended; to-wit, the nourishment of the said sick, wounded or convalescent soldiers (120–21).

Writing in this manner, the doctor was able to string out his report for twenty-four pages "and didn't say anything except that the bread was burnt in cooking."

Daniel held no grudges against the Yankees. In fact, in one of the few scenes in which he treats the enemy directly, his life is saved by a Union soldier. He had held up his handkerchief to indicate surrender, but evidently the Yanks didn't know what that meant, he says, because they kept shooting at him. He adds parenthetically that "it was a clean handkerchief, or I would not have much blamed them for not recognizing it." Anyway, he saw that his only chance was to roll over and play dead. This he did; whereupon a Yank came up, took him prisoner, and saved his life (134–41).

The small amount of satire in the book is mild and is directed toward soldiers who tried to stay away from the front lines by pleading sickness. One shirker, he remembers, described his illness this way: "Well, Doc . . . I mostly don't know 'zackly what ails me. I've got a misery in my chest, a soreness in my jints, a-a-kinder stiffness in my back, and hurtin' al-l-l over!" (152). The Old Doctor recalls that he once told the "chief . . . medicine-giver of ward three" to go back to his regiment "and tell your colonel to make you head chief, medical or otherwise, bullet-arrester; you'll be good to stop a bullet from some less important person" (157).

An anecdote of a dandy whom several ladies begged to sing for them incidentally exposed one of the most common ailments of the soldier. "'Oh, Miss Sue,—I cawn't sing, you know; only a little for my own amusement,' said this swell, with an air that, as Sut Lovingood would say, made my big toe itch; I felt like kicking him." Finally the dandy is persuaded and begins in his little falsetto voice. "W-h-y—am I so w-e-a-k and w-e-a-r-y—." At this point one of the graybacks shouts from a distance. "Hits 'cause you've got the di-ur-ree, you Sunday galoot!" (162).

The admiration of Southern belles made the hardships of war seem more bearable. In a poem obviously parodying Longfellow,

Daniel celebrated a roommate's alleged love affair. Entitled "The Clever Quartermaster; or the Fate of the Flirt," it begins:

> *Miss Maggie:*
> *Let me tell you a good story*
> *On my room-mate, Captain Riddle;*
> *Captain Riddle, Quartermaster*
> *Of the Post of Chattanooga;*
> *Riddle, with the auburn tresses*
> *All combed back so slick and shiney;*
> *Riddle, with the whiskers auburn,—(189–90).*

The Old Doctor also remembered fondly his own flirtations. One was with a Miss Vannie Vogle of Chattanooga, "the daintiest little darling of them all," who, when he first met her, would not say anything or even open her mouth. Deciding to take advantage of all opportunities, he tried to kiss her; but she broke away and ran to a porch where she "spat out a mouthful of brown juice." Looking at him reproachfully while wiping her mouth with the back of her hand, she said: "You fool—didn't you see I had snuff in my mouth?" (171). Fortunately, not all of his affairs were with snuff-dipping girls.

Though in his recollections the Old Doctor concentrated on the humorous side of the war, he was never unaware of its tragedy and deeper significance. Summing up his war experiences, he wrote: "But, upon the whole, I am glad I lived in wartimes. I trust to God that I may not live to see another war—but I am glad to have been through that one, and to have seen and experienced what I did" (259). Like most thinking survivors of the struggle, he understood the salutary effect on the nation; also like most, he preferred to think of its pleasant and amusing side.

Probably the most amusing and realistic reminiscences of the

Civil War were written by men who had fought in the ranks: "Sarge" Wier, Carlton McCarthy, William Fletcher, Sam Watkins, and others.

Sweet and Knox's *On a Mexican Mustang* touches on the Civil War soldier in several places.[3] A reporter who accompanies the two authors part of the way across Texas is a Confederate veteran and relates some of his amusing war experiences. One time, he says, the Yankees mistook a herd of cows for Rebel soldiers. "They trained two of the guns on the cattle while we were scattering. The cows, not having any more sense than we had, waited to be shelled. They staid there until the gunners got the range. We saw afterwards that the carnage was dreadful: tender-loin steaks and soup-bones were found scattered over the country for miles. We rejoiced that none of us were hurt: we did not wish to add to the bitterness of the fratricidal struggle" (497–98).

The reporter's war adventures are usually slapstick, and unlike Daniel's memoirs, have little significance outside farce. A representative adventure has to do with a pig-stealing scheme which misfires. Going from Texas through Louisiana by forced marches, "the first troops that went out from Texas were in very much of a hurry, because they feared that the war would be over before they could reach the tented field," they passed a farmer who was driving his pigs under the house for safekeeping. After camping for the night, the reporter and a buddy decided to go back and steal some fresh pork. With the reporter standing by the exit with a club, the ill-fated friend went under the house to drive the pigs out. Hearing a noise near the exit the reporter lammed a pig on the back of his head. The pig turned out to be his friend who was crawling out to tell him that the farmer had moved his live pork again. The reporter had hit his comrade-at-pig-stealing so hard, he had to carry him back to camp. The reporter commented: "From that hour I instinctively felt that the cause of the Confederacy was hopeless" (590–93).

A more significant memoir of the war is Sarge (A. M.) Wier's *Old Times in Georgia* (Atlanta, 1903). Wier's account of life in the ranks is much more realistic—sometimes grotesque—than most humorous memoirs. Although crudely written, Sarge's reminiscences smack of real life. For instance, he describes realistically the trouble he and three buddies had trying to divest a dead and stiff Union soldier of a new overcoat. Their difficulty was compounded because the corpse's arms were stretched out straight on either side. In Sarge's words: "They raised him on his feet and one of 'em got on one side and another on the other side and were trying to bend the stiff arms, when the fellow that was holding him up gave a quick jerk which turned the dead body and brought the stiff arms around with it and the open palm slapped Ned in the face, and it smacked as natural as if the yankee had er been alive and done it. Ned didn't stop to ask questions." In fact, the poor soldier didn't stop running until he got to camp; and no one could convince him he hadn't been hit by a ghost. From then on "he wouldn't have nothing to do with getting overcoats that way, and so he froze to death pretty soon after that, one night on picket" (4). Sarge's unaffected account of this incident tells more about the underclothed Confederate soldier than did reams of official reports in Richmond.

Sarge relates many realistic hospital stories of wartime. His telling about a young Texan who bled to death after a leg amputation reminds one of his auditors about his painful experience in a military hospital. As the war wore on, this man says, the draft age was raised and finally put him in the eligible category. He decided without hesitation that he had to develop a disqualifying ailment: "So the first thing you know my back was in such er bad fix that I couldn't move a chair from one side er the fireplace to the other, and it was soon norated all over the settlement that Brown's a plum invalid, and some 'lowed it was a spinal affection, and some 'lowed it was liftin' too much when I was young, and some 'lowed one thing and some 'lowed ernother, but me and the old 'oman and the gals knowed what it was" (9–10). Brown was safe until a conscript officer caught him carrying a big hickory log. Though he continued complaining about his back, he was taken in for a physical examination. Because of his alleged disorder he was sent to a hospital for a painful turpentine-burn cure. This treatment consisted of setting cups of burning turpentine on his bare back and then cutting the resultant blisters. After undergoing such an ordeal, Brown's condemnation of the medical profession is understandable. "I've hated hospitals and doctors from that day to this, and I always expect to."

Although Sarge is proud of war heroes like Lee, Jackson, and Longstreet, he constantly comments on the cruelty of war. He concludes that "war's er bad, bad thing" (37).

With the passage of time Charles H. Smith's bitter picture of the war mellowed. Eventually he came to see that not all Yankee soldiers had been villains, but he still preferred the South. In *Bill Arp: From the Uncivil War to Date 1861–1903* (Atlanta, 1903), his daughter wrote, "The Confederacy was a passion with my father. He loved to honor the old South and her veterans" (13).

In his old age, Smith wrote sentimentally of the war experiences of the original Bill Arp. After remarking that Arp had once stolen the general's apple brandy, he added a goodly portion of pathos: "He was a good soldier in war, the wit and wag of the camp fires, and made many a homesick youth laugh away his melancholy. He was a good citizen in peace. When told that his son was killed he looked no surprise, but simply said: 'Major, did he die all right?' When assured that he did, Bill wiped away a falling tear and said, with a choking voice: 'I only wanted to tell his mother'" (18). Smith had almost spent himself on war topics while the war was still being fought. When the clamor of Reconstruction died down, he restricted most of his writing to domestic subjects of the time.

In 1882, Carlton McCarthy, who had been a private in the army he wrote about, published in Richmond his *Detailed Minutiae of Soldier Life in the Army of Northern Virginia*, a eulogistic account of the Confederate soldier fighting against overpowering odds. Humor and pathos mix in this book of memoirs whose dominant mood is melancholy.

Like F. E. Daniel, McCarthy related how many a soldier's romantic notions about war were soon dispelled. Describing the typical soldier's outfit, which included an elaborately furnished knapsack and a haversack, he wrote, "It is amusing to think of the follies of the early part of the war, as illustrated by the outfits of the volunteers. They were so heavily clad, and so burdened with all manner of things, that a march was torture, and the wagon trains were so immense in proportion to the number of troops, that it would have been impossible to guard them in an enemy country. Subordinate officers thought themselves entitled to transportation for trunks, mattresses, and folding bedsteads, and the privates were as ridiculous in their demands" (19–20). Once the reality of war hit, they pared their baggage drastically until "reduced to the minimum, the private soldier consisted of one man, one hat, one jacket, one shirt, one pair of pants, one pair of drawers, one pair of shoes, and one pair of socks" (26).

Other romantic preconceptions of war quickly melted away. One was that soldiers should be as uncomfortable as possible and "glory in getting wet, being cold, hungry, and tired. So they refused shelter in houses or barns, and 'like true soldiers' paddled about in the mud and rain, thinking thereby to serve their country better" (30). Another quickly discarded notion was that one Confederate could whip a dozen Yankees. The former private admitted that this was "literally true sometimes, but, generally speaking, two to one made hard work for the boys" (32). Perhaps the most quickly rejected preconception of war was the belief that one should get wounded as soon as possible. "Many became despondent and groaned as they thought that perchance after all they were doomed to go home safe and sound, and hear, for all time, the praises of the fellow who had lost his arm by a cannon shot, or had his face ripped by a sabre, or his head smashed with a fragment of shell" (33). Men soon found out that getting wounded was the next thing to getting killed, and that often a simple "hero's" wound could prove fatal.

McCarthy's treatment of common soldier life is excellent. There is, for example, this almost perfect vignette: "An accomplished straggler could assume more misery, look more horribly emaciated, tell more dismal stories of distress, eat more and march further (to the rear), than any ten ordinary men" (54). Other glimpses of military low life include foraging raids on farmers' hog pens, corn fields, and cow pastures. Many of these raids terminated in hilarious failure. One rabbit hunt, without benefit of guns, however, ended in success—at least for one officer: "A faithful officer, worn out with the long, weary march, sick, hungry, and dejected, leaned his back against a tree and groaned to think of his inability to join in the chase of an old hare, which, he knew, from the wild yells in the wood, his men were pursuing. But the uproar approached him—nearer, nearer, and nearer, until he saw the hare bounding towards him with a regiment at her heels. She spied an opening made by the folds of the officer's cloak and jumped in, and he embraced his first meal for forty-eight hours" (70).

Some of McCarthy's humor seems related to the coarse antebellum humor. "An artilleryman, camped for a day where no water was to be found easily, awakened during the night by thirst, went stumbling about in search of water; and to his great delight found a large bucketful. He drank his fill, and in the morning found that what he drank had washed a bullock's head, and was crimson with its blood" (70–71). He also tells of several stragglers who came into camp one night and found a large pot of soup which they drank, although it tasted peculiar. The next morning they checked to see what had given it the odd taste and found that it had been "strongly impregnated with the peculiar flavor of defunct cockroaches." The author also remembers having eaten rats. A muskrat was "skinned, cleaned, buried a day or two, disinterred, cooked, and eaten with great relish" (71).

Chapter VII, "Fun and Fury on the Field," concerns the cheering, laughter, fun, and pathos of battle. Describing a battle scene as an on-the-spot witness, McCarthy wrote: "As we approach, a ludicrous scene presents itself. A strong-armed artilleryman is energetically thrashing a dejected looking individual with a hickory bush, and urging him to the front. He has managed to keep out of many a fight, but now he *must* go in. The captain has detailed a man to *whip* him in, and the man is doing it. With every blow the poor fellow yells and begs to be spared, but his determined guardian will not cease. They press on, the one screaming and the other lashing, till they reach the battery in position and firing on the retiring enemy" (99–100).

McCarthy proved that even the heat of battle is occasion for humor. He told of a big brawny fellow who at Gettysburg, when the artillery fire was at its height, burst out singing "Backward, roll backward, O Time in thy flight: Make me a child again, just for this *fight!*" A fellow near him interrupted with "Yes; and a *gal* child at that" (106–107).

The ex-Rebel could even find humor in defeat. During a retreat a Southern artilleryman was approached by a Yankee cavalryman who shouted for him to surrender. The Reb didn't stop. The Yank became indignant and shouted, "Halt, d—n you; halt!" Still the Reb continued to walk. "Halt," repeated the cavalryman furiously, "halt, you d—n s—of a———; halt!" That did it. "Then the artilleryman halted, and remarking that he didn't allow any man to speak to *him* that way, seized a huge stick, turned on the cavalryman, knocked him out of his saddle, and proceeded on his journey to the rear" (114).

ANOTHER AMUSING ACCOUNT OF low life in the Confederate army is William Andrew Fletcher's *Rebel Private Front and Rear* (Austin, 1954). Born in Louisiana, Fletcher moved with his family to Texas, where he enlisted in the Confederate army when the war started. His delightful sense of humor is evident throughout the record of his war experiences. The style of *Rebel Private* is unpolished but lively.

Fletcher remembered that he had a hard time staying healthy enough to fight in the war. On arrival at Richmond he found that he had a case of measles. Then he developed the itch, which actually turned out to be body lice. After that he came down with the mumps. When he recovered from that, he slipped from a persimmon tree and had to return to the hospital. Finally he had an attack of jaundice. When he at last recovered from all these maladies, he was ready for service.

At least he thought he was ready for service, until another health specter haunted him in camp: diarrhea. In the following words he records his meeting with this malady and the cure he found for it: "I, with a number of others, had quite an amusing experience—with a happy ending—and it was this: We were sufferers from camp diarrhea, as it was called, and up to that time we had found no cure. So, entering the battle, I had quite a great fear that something disgraceful might happen and it was somewhat uppermost in my mind; but to my surprise the excitement, or something else, had effected a cure. I inquired of some of the others and they reported a cure" (15–16).

The most that can be said for the Rebel private's humor connected with food is that it is mildly nauseating. For example, until Fletcher discovered a cat's claw in his portion, sausage was a favorite dish with the men. His description of animals to be slaughtered and the meat taken from them is, to say the least, unpalatable:

> In every brute there was depicted the wanting condition of the owner. The once pride of the family was slowly but surely starving to death and the end was near, for there were numbers that one would think when they lay down that they never would rise again until skinned and carted away to their last resting place—the soldier's stomach. The most of this meat, when cooked, would turn to jelly and one would think of sweetening. It was not necessary to have a peg to hang it on—throw it against a tree and it would stick. Need not necessarily be a nearby tree, as there was little danger of its being stolen, as each fellow had enough of the kind. After being thrown against the tree it had the appearance of some hideous picture of a sea monster trying to climb down, as the tendons would stick where they came in contact with the tree and would slowly stretch from the weight of body whether the entire piece would go to strings, or not. We never made a test, but I have often pulled meat off—if such it could be called—when the meat was from two to four inches below where it first stuck. If the reader of this undertakes to make test to prove the correctness of this statement, I would ask him to go for his material where he can get fair samples under like conditions. Here was where it was reported that some men ate the unborn calf if it was spotted. This word "spotted" was to denote one that had the hair on (71–72).

Typical of the memoirs written by foot soldiers, *Rebel Private* relates in serio-comic exaggeration the deprivations of the war.

Fletcher's humor is sometimes almost Freudian. One can only wonder what he had in mind when he reported the following scene on a visit to a Yankee infirmary: "I was somewhat amused, however, with one fine-looking, intelligent young fellow, who, from appearances and conversation, had lived on the bright side of life; he was on his feet and slowly moving about; he said, 'Reb, look what you fellows have done for me. I would rather that bullet had gone through my head, and I guess my girl will hunt another fellow when she hears of it'" (38–39).

Another time his humor seems to border on the sadistic. He and a friend see a mass of moving people—Yankee soldiers and Negro civilians mixed in—and decide to have a little fun by firing on the mounted enemy, "not caring a straw whether we hit a negro or not." He recalls the scene with macabre humor: "We turned loose with our carbines, three charges each—terror reigned, and there was as if by magic, a dismounting, jumping from carts and wagons; and I guess there were a number of mothers who forgot their babies, and grandmas and grandpas who forgot, for the time, that there was such a thing as rheumatism" (90).

In addition to being at least semi-sadistic—he liked to tease cowards in battle—Fletcher must have been a tough and brave soldier. Remembering an operation on a serious wound in his hip, he writes, "Without further question they commenced to cut and from the way the knife pulled the muscle, I took it to be very dull, and was expressing my views in very forcible terms when one of them remarked: 'If you don't hush up we will leave you.' My reply was, 'It don't hurt as badly when I am cursing'" (43). He recalls, however, a medicine he once tried to no avail. "While in the line, I thought of my gin and opened a bottle, and the most of the boys did the same. I was not used to drink, but wanted to test gin as a fear tonic; so I partook of the remedy freely, but the bullets would make about the same impression at each visitation, and when we were marched off, the most of one bottle was gone and the bullets sounded the same old way" (141–42).

Foraging was as much a necessity in Fletcher's outfit as in

McCarthy's. Corn patches, beehives, and hen houses were especially attractive objects of foraging expeditions. Chicken-stealing was reduced by hungry soldiers to a science. The following directions, devised by an old Negro, are guaranteed by Fletcher to work "where chickens roost low":

> When you get under their roost, let the chickens get through with their low croaking, and stop operations—if they do hear something and start it again, wait till all is quiet and commence again. Put your hand on the roost (back up is best), move it along the roost until you touch a foot; the chicken will raise up, slip your hand under and when he puts his foot down on your hand, you will know about the size of the chicken and direction of its head. If you don't want the chicken, or its head is toward you, turn your hand and draw from under its foot and the chicken will put its foot back on the roost. If you want the fowl, change so your hand will be on the other side of the roost. This will put its head from you. Repeat operation and when one foot is on your hand, slowly slip your hand to touch the other foot and it will raise and put that foot on your hand. When both feet are on your hand, raise a little, then when the chicken's body is clear of the roost, lower gently, at the same time swing across breast and raise left arm at the shoulder. When chicken's body is under, give quick up motion with chicken and downward clamp with your arm. As you are doing this, grab the neck with left hand, and with the other hand clamp its head, give a twist and pull and neck is broken. Hold for a moment—this hard squeezing and lack of freedom to flutter will quiet the nerve instantly. Holding by head, lower the chicken until ground is touched and turn loose. If on the floor, hold to the head till it touches the floor. This can be repeated as often as wished, and the darker the night the better, as the owner cannot peep through

> a crack and see you, and as he hears nothing he would at once leave, and if light is seen, one has time to creep away (57–58).

This method worked for Flecher and many others during the war, but he had his reservations about its practicality in the electric age. He concluded: "I guess one would be less at ease now, for the electric snap light would be on his mind."

On the way home to Texas after the surrender, Fletcher stopped for lodging at a house infested with rats. In the concluding pages of his memoirs he describes how he helped rid the house of the vermin by putting a sack over a rat hole and running the rats into it. The work was interrupted only briefly when a rat ran up a girl's dress. Once home in Beaumont he applied for work at the sawmill where he had worked for thirty-five dollars a month plus room and board before the war. He was offered sixteen dollars to do the same work, but declined saying, "Four years lost and wages cut." There was only one resort left him: "So I went home and gathered up father's old carpenter tools and went on a job at a dollar and a half a day, about one hundred feet from the place where I left off work" (158).

ONE OF THE MOST delightful memoirs of the war is Sam R. Watkins's *Co. Aytch: A Confederate Memoir of the Civil War,* written in 1881–82 and published first in the Columbia, Tennessee, *Herald.*[4] At a time when most popular writers were romanticizing the war, Watkins wrote with surprising realism. Some of his Rebel soldiers drink, gamble, swear; some are cowards. Since he wrote from memory, some of his facts are inaccurate. Another limitation is his coolness toward Yankees, which sometimes breaks through when he recounts war atrocities. But all in all the book is vigorous and readable. One of the book's dominating features is its humor. Writing in the "Introduction" to the reprint of 1952, Bell Irvin Wiley says: "Soldiering also had its brighter side, and it is in presenting this aspect that Watkins is at his best. His humor is so irrepressible that it frequently breaks through the most serious passages to blend mirth with tragedy" (19). The critic concludes his commentary with this judgment: "No memoir by a Rebel participant is richer in intimate detail of common soldier life than this engaging story told by Private Sam R. Watkins of the First Tennessee."[5]

Watkins himself limited his scope by explaining that he was not writing a history, but merely the observations of a private in the rear ranks of the army. History tells of the great men and events of war, "But in the following pages I propose to tell of the fellows who did the shooting and killing, the fortifying and ditching, the sweeping of the streets, the drilling, the standing guard, picket and videt, and who drew (or were to draw) eleven dollars per month and rations, and also drew the ramrod and tore the cartridge" (47).

The satiric tone of much of the book appears early when Watkins, in discussing the events that led to the war, spoke of the leaders of the two sides. Of President Lincoln and Vice President Hannibal Hamlin he wrote: "The other side selected as captain a son of Nancy Hanks, of Bowling Green, and a son of old Bob Lincoln, the rail-splitter, and whose name was Abe. Well, after he was elected captain, they elected as first lieutenant an individual of doubtful blood by the name of Hannibal Hamlin, being a descendant of the generation of Ham, the bad son of old Noah, who meant to curse him blue, but overdid the thing, and cursed him black" (46).

Satire also colors the author's handling of officers and even noncommissioned officers. Once, he says, after a battle he noticed that the military hierarchy from corporals to captains had torn all the fine lace off their uniforms. When he asked several why they had done this, their reply was: "Humph, you think that I was going to be a target for the Yankees to shoot at?" Watkins comments caustically: "You see, this was our first battle, and the officers had not found out that minnie as well as cannon balls were blind; that they had no eyes and could not see. They thought that the balls would hunt for them and not hurt the privates. I always shot at privates. It was they that did the shooting and killing, and if I could kill or wound a private, why, my chances were so much the better. I always looked upon officers as harmless personages" (55).

Scenes of stark realism and grotesqueness that are the antithesis of typical postwar treatments are frequently inserted by Watkins. He remembers the time in Virginia he was with a group which went to relieve a guard unit: "If I remember correctly, there were just eleven of them. Some were sitting down and some were lying down; but each and every one was as cold and as hard frozen as the icicles that hung from their hands and faces and clothing—dead! They had died at their post on duty. Two of them, a little in advance of the others, were standing with their guns in their hands, as cold and as hard frozen as a monument of marble—standing sentinel with loaded guns in their frozen hands!" (62). His description of the Chickamauga battlefield the day after the battle could not be made more gory: "Men were lying where they fell, shot in every conceivable part of the body. Some with their entrails torn out and still hanging to them and piled up on the ground beside them, and they still alive. Some with their underjaw torn off, and hanging by a fragment of skin to their cheeks, with their tongues lolling from their mouth, and they trying to talk. Some with both eyes shot out, and with one eye hanging down on their cheek. In fact, you might walk over the battlefield and find men shot from the crown of the head to the tip end of the toe" (118–19). There is probably no scene in the work of prewar humorists with realism this vivid. Other passages in *Co. Aytch* are just as bloody. Watkins told of a cannon ball that tore a buddy's head off, "splattering his brains all over my face and bosom," and of visiting an Atlanta hospital and seeing in the rear of the building "a pile of arms and legs, rotting and decomposing."

Desertion was a perennial problem in the Confederate army. Watkins recalled with horror the punishments meted out to deserters and to men who had gone AWOL. Deserters were often shot, and AWOLers were usually whipped unmercifully and branded in full view of their comrades. "And when some miserable wretch was to be whipped and branded for being absent ten days without leave, we had to see him kneel down and have his head shaved smooth and slick as a peeled onion, and then stripped to the naked skin. Then a strapping fellow with a big rawhide would make the blood flow and spurt at every lick, the wretch begging and howling like a hound, and then he was branded with the letter D on both hips, when he was marched through the army to the music of the 'Rogue's March'" (71).

Even in the midst of describing a battle Watkins would pause to insert an anecdote. He remembers, for example, a funny incident during the Battle of Shiloh. "As we advanced, on the edge of the battlefield, we saw a big fat colonel of the 23rd Tennessee regiment badly wounded, whose name, if I remember correctly, was Matt. Martin. He said to us, 'Give 'em goss, boys. That's right, my brave First Tennessee. Give 'em Hail Columbia!' We halted but a moment, and said I, 'Colonel, where are you wounded?' He answered in a deep bass voice, 'My son, I am wounded in the arm, in the leg, in the head, in the body, and in another place which I have a delicacy in mentioning'" (65).

No memoir of common soldier life was ever complete without mention of one pestilence that afflicted just about every man. Watkins wrote, "Every soldier had a brigade of lice on him, and I have seen fellows so busily engaged in cracking them that it reminded me of an old woman knitting." At first, he says, the men were embarrassed when they discovered they had lice and would go off by themselves into the woods to delouse; but when they found out that almost everybody was crawling with the little vermin, they lost their self-consciousness. "Pharaoh's people, when they were resisting old Moses, never enjoyed the curse of lice more than we did." Entertainments built around lice became popular, with louse races common everywhere. Watkins recalled the champion louse racer in his outfit: "There was one fellow who was winning all the money; his lice would run quicker and crawl faster than anybody's lice. We could not understand it. If some fellow happened to catch a fierce-looking louse, he would call on Dornin for a race. Dornin would come and always win the stake. The lice were placed in plates—this was the race course—and the first that crawled off was the winner. At last we found out Dornin's trick; he always heated his plate" (76).[6]

Although occasionally harsh on the Yankees, Watkins is usually objective when he mentions the enemy. Before the battle at Perryville he stood picket duty on one side of the street in the town with a Yankee picket within talking distance on the other side. They got quite chummy that night "and made a raid upon a citizen's pantry, where we captured a bucket of honey, a pitcher of sweet milk, and three or four biscuit" (81). The next day they were trying to kill each other. Another time he tried to rob a dead Yankee. "In passing over the battlefield [at Murfreesboro], I came across a dead Yankee colonel. He had on the finest clothes I ever saw, a red sash and fine sword. I particularly noticed his boots. I needed them, and had made up my mind to wear them out for him. But I could not bear the thought of wearing dead men's shoes. I took hold of the foot and raised it up and made one trial at the boot to get it off. I happened to look up, and the colonel had his eyes wide open, and seemed to be looking at me. He was stone dead, but I dropped that foot quick" (95). After relating that grotesque experience, Watkins adds, "It was my first and last attempt to rob a dead Yankee." Other men were not so squeamish.

The only time the author mentions specifically killing anyone, he shows regret. He recalls painfully that his victim "was the prettiest youth I ever saw. When I fired, the Yankees broke and run, and I went up to the boy I had killed, and the blood was gushing out of his mouth. I was sorry" (195).

Almost everyone in the army, he writes, had a nickname—from generals down to privates. Had the war lasted ten years, "we would have forgotten our proper names" (89). Common nicknames included Sneak, Apple Jack, Devil Horse, Old Snake, Greasy, Buzzard, Hog, and Brutus.

Practical jokes, always popular among the common people of the South, flourished during the war. Larking, or snipe-hunting, was a favorite. Watkins described the way it was done in the army. "The way to go 'a larking' is this: Get an empty meal bag and about a dozen men and go to some dark forest or open field on some cold, dark, frosty or rainy night, about five miles from camp. Get someone who does not understand the game to hold the bag in as stooping and cramped a position as is possible, to keep perfectly still and quiet, and when he has got in the right fix, the others to go off to drive in the larks. As soon as they get out of sight, they break in a run and go back to camp, and go to sleep, leaving the poor fellow all the time holding the bag" (106–7). Watkins was party to a larking expedition, but later regretted having taken part when the sleepy-eyed and exhausted young greenhorn brought his bag back to him the next morning.

When foraging didn't supplement their food stores sufficiently, soldiers often had to resort to other devices. Watkins recalled a time when he and several other hungry men caught a large rat in an old outhouse. "We skinned him, washed and salted him, buttered and peppered him, and fried him. He actually looked nice. The delicate aroma of the frying rat came to our hungry nostrils. We were keen to eat a piece of rat; our teeth were on edge; yea, even our mouth watered for a piece of rat. Well, after a while, he was said to be done. I got a piece of cold corn dodger, laid my piece of rat on it, ate a little piece of bread, and raised the piece of rat to my mouth, when I happened to think of how that rat's tail did slip. I had lost my appetite for dead rat. I did not eat any rat. It was my first and last effort to eat dead rat" (108–9).

Usually a soldier had to do his own laundry, but occasionally he could find a colored woman near camp to do it for him. Watkins found such a washerwoman in Aunt Daphne, whose husband, Uncle Zack—when awake—would entertain him with his talk about his religion. One time Uncle Zack told him about the night the devil visited him and took him to hell. Once in hell the devil "jes stretch a wire across hell, and hang me up jes same like a side of bacon, through the tongue." As the old Negro continued, his memory became more vivid: "Well, dar I hang like de bacon, and de grease kept droppin' down and would blaze up all 'round me. I jes stay dar and burn; and after while de debil come 'round wid his gun, and say, 'Zack, I gwine to shoot you,' and jes as he raise de gun, I jes jerk loose from dat wire, and I jes fly to heben." Watkins then began questioning Uncle Zack about his experiences in heaven.

> "Fly! did you have wings?"
>
> "O, yes, sir, I had wings."
>
> "Well, after you got to heaven, what did you do then?"
>
> "Well, I jes went to eatin' grass like all de balance of de lams."
>
> "What! were they eating grass?"
>
> "O, yes, sir."
>
> "Well, what color were the lambs, Uncle Zack?"
>
> "Well, sir, some of dem was white, and some black, and some spotted."
>
> "Were there no old rams or ewes among them?"
>
> "No, sir; dey was all lams."

> "Well, Uncle Zack, what sort of a looking lamb were you?"
>
> "Well, sir, I was sort of specklish and brown like."
>
> Old Zack begins to get sleepy.
>
> "Did you have horns, Uncle Zack?"
>
> "Well, some of dem had little horns dat look like dey was jes sorter sproutin' like."
>
> Zack begins to nod and doze a little.
>
> "Well, how often did they shear the lambs, Uncle Zack?"
>
> "Well, w-e-l-l, w—e—l—l," and Uncle Zack was fast asleep and dreaming no doubt of the beautiful pastures glimmering above the clouds of heaven (140–41).

Such interludes must have provided Watkins with comic relief from the worries of warfare.

Watkins came out of the army only one notch above the rank he went in. Ironically, the only promotion he ever got was for breaking ranks and picking up a deserted flag. He comments mock-seriously, "And had I only known that picking up flags entitled me to promotion and that every flag picked up would raise me one notch higher, I would have quit fighting and gone to picking up flags, and by that means I would have soon been President of the Confederate States of America" (180). Thousands of readers have been glad that he stuck to being a private; otherwise there would be no *"Co. Aytch."* Without Watkins's book and other humorous memoirs of the war, our knowledge of the period would be sadly incomplete.

The reunited nation delighted to read anecdotes of Civil War soldiers—great and lowly. Many of the stories were apocryphal, but truth (or lack of it) did not bother a people busy making Stonewall Jackson, Jeb Stuart, and the common soldier into legends. Rare was the book written about the war which failed to include a section variously called "Humors of the Camp." "Comic Aspects of Battle," or "The Light Side of the War."

The novelist and former Confederate captain, John Esten Cooke, wrote in *Camp-Fire Sketches*: "The humorous side of the drama may be less inspiring and exciting, but it is more amusing and characteristic . . . the main object is to show how men in positions of grave responsibility, enough to crush out all tendency to fun, yet showed a marked tendency to enjoy the 'sunny side' of things, and laugh when ruin itself stared them in the face."[7]

While Cooke was occupied writing down the humor of Stuart and Jackson, another chronicler of Civil War humor, W. W. Blackford, had an amusing story to tell about Cooke. In a section of *War Years with Jeb Stuart* entitled "Captain Cooke Dodges a Shell," he records a comic incident at the Battle of Mechanicsville:

> While we were all sitting on our horses in a conspicuous part of the field, a battery noticed us by a round. One of the shots passed screaming a few inches over our heads. We were not so well accustomed to artillery then as we became afterwards, and most of us involuntarily ducked our heads. Capt. John Esten Cooke, while so doing, bowed a little too low, lost his balance, and fell sprawling on the ground. We were all a good deal shocked, for we did not doubt for a moment that his head had been carried off. Stuart leaned down from his saddle and in a most sympathizing voice said, "Hallo, Cooke! Are you hit?" But Cooke jumped up looking very sheepish as he dusted himself and said, "Oh, no, General; I only dodged a little too far." The reaction of feeling from the uneasiness we had felt for him, and his ludicrous appearance as he scrambled back into his saddle, still covered with dust, was perfectly irresistible, and we laughed until we could scarcely keep our seats in our saddles. For months after, almost every time Cooke appeared at the breakfast table, the General would call to him, "Hallo, Cooke! Are you hit?" or

> "No, General; I only dodged too far." He [Stuart] loved a joke, and would ring the changes on one until a better one turned up (73–74).

A Confederate general as admired as Stonewall Jackson was bound to figure in many humorous stories. One anecdote in which Jackson was involved shows the adulation the Southerner accorded his military leaders. A Virginia planter had given almost all he had to the Confederacy; he had kept for his own use only one ten-acre lot of corn. One day he was exasperated to see a troop of cavalry riding through his corn, and he angrily threatened to report them to President Davis. But when he discovered that their leader was Stonewall Jackson, he changed his tone completely and babbled excitedly: "God bless you, General Jackson! I am so glad to see you! Go back and ride all over my field, damn you, ride all over my field! Get down, and come into my house. I am so glad to see you. Ride all over my field, all over it—all over it! Bless your soul, I'm so glad to see you."[8]

Jackson's men admired him extravagantly, too. Because he said he liked the taste of whiskey too much, he was a teetotaler; but this prohibition did not extend to his men, who drank frequent toasts to him. These two subjects are combined in the following anecdote about Jackson: "On one occasion, a soldier who had imbibed enthusiasm with his whiskey, feeling the inadequacy of the devotion shown by drinking to an absent chief, marched, canteen in hand, to Jackson's tent, and gaining admission, proposed as a sentiment, 'Here's to you, General! May I live to see you stand on the highest pinnacle of Mount Ararat, and hear you give the command, "By the right of nations front into empires,—worlds, right face!"'"[9]

The Yankees contributed to making Jackson into a legend. It was widely believed among Union soldiers, for example, that Stonewall never slept. The Yanks had good reason to place his powers above those of the average man, for time and again he maneuvered his troops for coups that startled both sides. One of Cooke's anecdotes about Jackson contains as much truth as humor. He wrote that when Jackson was told that General McClellan was close by with a large army, he asked if the Yanks had many beef cattle with them. When he was told yes, he said with a dry smile: "Well, I can whip any army that comes well supplied with beef cattle!"[10] Jackson's insistence on strict discipline also contributed to the building of his legend. Sam Watkins said of him: "He did his duty himself and was ever at his post, and he expected and demanded of everybody to do the same thing. He would have a man shot at the drop of a hat, and drop it himself."[11]

Although many of the heaviest burdens of the war fell on Robert E. Lee, even he was not without humor. Biographies of Lee almost always include incidents which show breaks in his gravity. One anecdote concerns the time at Petersburg when he visited one of his major generals and in the course of the talk asked about the condition of his subordinate's lines. The man told him they were in good shape, but when they visited the lines, they found no work had been done. Noticing the spirited horse the major general was riding, Lee suggested in the following words a remedy for both the lines and the horse: "I would suggest to you that *these rough paths along these trenches would be very admirable ground over which to tame him.*"[12] Cooke recorded an incident during the Chancellorsville campaign when a young officer rode up in haste to report to Lee that the Yanks had attacked. Smiling, Lee is supposed to have said, "Well, I heard firing, and I was beginning to think it was time some of you lazy fellows were coming to tell me what it was all about."[13]

Cooke also vouched for the humor of General Fitzhugh Lee. "He was full of humor, as brave as steel, without any 'official dignity' whatever in his manner, but at all times the hearty soldier, loving his jest dearly and never in low spirits, whatever the outlook might be." Cooke also reported that Fitzhugh Lee once told him that his great ambition was "to have a company of Negro minstrels this winter—all mulattoes" (567–69). Thus was humor helping to romanticize and legendize Southern war heroes.

Other popular war figures in humor were Colonel W. H. F. Lee; General Richard Ewell, whose humor was generally profane; and the daring raider, Captain John Morgan. But the Southern patriot with by far the greatest reputation for humor was General Jeb Stuart. Cooke called him "the gayest probably of all the Southern generals" and noted that his staff consisted chiefly of young men who loved fun. The General's banjo player accompanied him everywhere. Cooke reported a meeting between Stuart and a former West Point classmate while the former was on a reconnaissance mission in 1861. Stuart said to his former friend, "I didn't know you were on our side," to which his companion responded by pointing to his command, a Federal battery just coming into sight. They both had a good laugh over the confusion and went back to their respective sides (555). From then until the end of the war Stuart's humor figured in stories told from the Potomac to the Rio Grande.

Blackford idolized his commander and recorded many instances of Stuart's love of humor. Sometimes Stuart was but a laughing observer, as in the following anecdote:

> Once during the night I had an adventure with a dog which amused General Stuart and my comrades of the staff no little, though it was not at all amusing to me. Passing a country house, General Stuart told me to go in and find out if the man had seen or heard anything of the enemy. He waited at the gate of the yard while I dismounted and went in. The house stood fifty yards from the road, and half way to it a large bulldog dashed out and made a furious attack upon me. We were now very near

> the camps of the enemy and it would not do to use fire-arms, so I received the dog on the point of my sabre, inflicting a wound in the shoulder which, though arresting his first attack, placed him upon his guard and only infuriated him the more. He circled round and round just out of reach of my thrusts, uttering savage growls which showed plainly enough what he would do if he could get hold of me with his teeth. Stuart roared with laughter and called out continually, "Give it to him, Blackford," for he had an instinctive love of fighting and enjoyed seeing the battle, and but for the order about firearms I would have made quick work of it with my pistol.[14]

As much of the humor in this sketch comes from the *way* Blackford relates it as from the incident itself, though comic it surely must have been when Stuart witnessed it. According to Blackford, when Stuart was almost captured by the enemy at Verdiersville, he lost his hat and haversack to them, much to the amusement of his troops. But the General retaliated in kind a few days later when he captured General Pope's coat and hat at Catlett's Station. Later when Pope's headquarters was captured, a full dress uniform belonging to the Federal general was brought to Stuart, who sent it to a friend in Richmond. There the uniform was displayed in a bookstore with a card which read: "Headquarters in the Saddle" and "The Rear Taking Care of Itself" (97–98).

Stuart's recklessness was the subject of many humorous stories. Eggleston wrote of one of the General's daring performances, "after capturing a large number of horses and mules on one of his raids, he seized a telegraph station and sent a dispatch to General Meigs, then Quartermaster-General of the United States army, complaining that he could not afford to come after animals of so poor a quality, and urging that officer to provide better ones for capture in the future."[15] In spurring his men on, Stuart made frequent use of his humor. Blackford told of an incident in which Stuart, passing by some men who told him they had been on picket duty for thirty-six hours without food, gave the men a little pep talk which made them forget their hunger: "Oh nonsense! You don't look starved. There's a cornfield over there; jump the fence and get a good breakfast. You don't want to go back to camp, I know; it's stupid there, and all the fun is out here. I never go to camp if I can help it. Besides, I've kept your company on duty all this time as a compliment" (134–35). Although this incident was related as a humorous story, the General meant his words to be taken seriously. The compliment he paid the men was a genuine one.

Cooke recorded the time Stuart made horse sense sound humorous. Once when an officer reported to him that his command must fall back because a rain had dampened their powder and made their guns useless, Stuart told him, "No . . . hold your ground. If the rain wets your powder it will wet your enemy's, too." In conclusion, Cooke wrote, "He made a frolic of war, in fact, and nothing ever seemed to cast him down or made him in the least doubtful of the result. He was always laughing, paying compliments to ladies, or roaring out his camp songs when he was not fighting hard, or working hour after hour at his desk" (560–62). At the head of his marching column Stuart would amuse some of his men—and terrify some—by singing such songs as: "If you get there before I do, Oh, tell 'em I'm a-coming too!" Stuart could agree with Joel Chandler Harris, who once said that humor was a good thing to die by.

Foreign soldiers sent to the South by their governments as observers were occasionally the source of much amusement because of their old-world attitudes and their strange accents. A Prussian assigned to Jeb Stuart's staff, Major Heros Von Borcke, entertained his Southern comrades with his antics. In *War Years with Jeb Stuart* Blackwood devoted more space to Von Borcke's theatrics than to many critical battles (156–60). He related one of the Prussian's entertainments held in a private home before Stuart and his staff. A sheet was stretched across the hall against which the shadows of the actors were cast. When the scene opened, Von Borcke was sitting on a couch dressed in a large nightshirt stuffed with pillows. He began to groan, and a nurse appeared and sent for a doctor. A ridiculously dressed doctor came in and gave the patient a deep draught from a bottle, "and then, on the sly, the doctor takes one too, to the great delight of the audience." Between groans of agony the patient managed to tell the doctor the things he'd just eaten at a dinner party. To relieve him, the doctor reached down his throat (or appeared to) and "pulls out in succession, and holds up for inspection, a pair of deer's horns, some beef's horns, cabbages, stalks and all, quantities of oyster shells, etc., etc., and finally a pair of boots." At each delivery an assistant took out a pillow from Von Borcke's nightshirt, and the patient uttered excruciating cries of relief—until finally he was considered cured. He then jumped up, embraced the doctor, and the two began "swigging at the bottle of physic . . . until they become tipsy, and the performance closes in an uproarious dance of doctor and patient. . . ." Blackford concluded his account with this critique: "The wit and humor displayed in this performance I have rarely seen equalled and its effect on the audience was convulsive. All the negroes on the place were allowed to come in to see it and their intense appreciation of the scene, and their rich, broad peals of laughter added no little to its attractions."

Another hilarious performance recorded by Blackford had Von Borcke playing the part of a blushing maiden. The sketch showed an Irishman courting his sweetheart. This is Blackford's description of Paddy's beloved: "Von Borcke was transformed into a blushing maiden weighing two hundred and fifty pounds and six feet two and a half inches tall; a riding skirt of one of the girls, supplemented by numerous dainty underskirts and extended by enormous hoops according to the fashion then in vogue, hung in graceful folds to conceal the huge cavalry boots the huge damsel wore. Her naturally ample bosom palpitated under skillfully arranged pillows, and was gorgeously decorated with . . . jewelry and ribbons, while 'a love of a bonnet,' long braids of hair, and quantities of powder and rouge completed her toilet, and in her hand she flirted coquettishly a fan of huge dimensions." Von Borcke's suitor was a colonel dressed as an Irishman, complete with red nose. As the two promenaded around the room arm-in-arm they made comic love conversation. Their disguises were so good no one suspected their identity. Only when they began to waltz and the maiden's hoop skirts flew up "that twinkling amid the white drapery beneath, the well-known boots of Von Borcke betrayed the first suspicion of who the lady was." And then "as suddenly as they had come they vanished, waltzing out through the open door and followed by convulsive roars of laughter from the delighted audience."

The Prussians seem to have sent over a battalion of observers, for another amusing Prussian attached to the Southern army was a Captain Scheibert, a man with artistic as well as military talents and the subject of several comic sketches by Blackford. One episode deals with the time the fat little foreigner agreed to aid Mrs. W. H. F. Lee, visiting her husband near an encampment, in touching up an oil sketch of "a small-size female head" which she had just finished. When they had finished working on the portrait, they placed it on a chair to dry. Later during an animated conversation the Prussian accidentally—and unknown to himself or anyone else—sat down in the chair that held the wet picture. Blackford described the scene:

> When the time came for him to go Mrs. Lee thanked him cordially, and told him she would keep the picture as a souvenir of their pleasant acquaintance, and turned to get the picture for him to take a last critical survey of it. Where was the picture?

> "Bless my soul!" said the Captain, "I laid it down on one of the chairs, but I don't see it now." Then they looked and looked. "Oh!" said Scheibert, "the wind must have blown it under the piano!" "Here it is," said Mrs. Lee, screaming with laughter, as she peeled the unfortunate picture from the broad seat of Scheibert's white trousers, leaving the lovely face, somewhat blurred, transferred thereto most conspicuously.
>
> Scheibert backed out from under the piano and without taking leave, or stopping to get his hat, cane and gloves in the hall, bolted across the fields for our camp. We saw him coming, waving his arms wildly and roaring like a bull with laughter. He threw himself on the grass, still convulsed, rolling over and over, and every time he turned that side up there was a bright picture of a lovely face on the seat of his trousers. It was a long time before he could find breath to tell us about it, and then you may rest assured we enjoyed the joke (207–8).

Blackford's light touch and deft style have preserved well the original humor of the episode.

Of the other amusing incidents in which Scheibert is a central character, one of the best is Blackford's account of the Prussian's poor horsemanship, "a never-ending source of amusement to us." Scheibert's sloppy habit of tying his belongings to his saddle with strings and straps often caused him to lose items. Once given an order by Stuart to deliver to authorize reinforcements, he "in his headlong impulsive way dashed off with it at full speed, but to Stuart's horror took by mistake a road which led directly towards the enemy." The General quickly ordered a courier to try to catch him before he reached the Yankees; but Scheibert, seeing a horseman following him, mistook him for an enemy and spurred his horse on faster, with a bundle coming loose at nearly every jump of his horse. Fortunately the courier intercepted him just short of the enemy lines. Blackford ends: "To retrace their steps and find the scattered property was no easy task but poor Captain Scheibert at last appeared, sadly crestfallen and greatly to the relief of Stuart's mind" (208–9).

Humorous stories by the thousands—some true, some half true, and some lies—were chronicled about lesser known men. Daniel's *Rebel Surgeon*, for example, tells of an engineer officer who demonstrated to a group of gullible officers that a toad could swallow coals of fire without harm. Catching a large toad, he then sent his colored boyservant for some live coals and prepared for the exhibition: "He went cautiously towards the toad, and with thumb and finger thumped a live coal right plump in the frog's path—right before his face. Well, sirs, that old toad stopped, straightened up, turned his head on one side and took a square look at the coal. It must have been just what he was looking for, as he seemed pleased to meet it. His eyes shone with a new light, and he made a grab at the coal and swallowed it with apparent relish. Fact. His eyes sparkled still more, and beyond doubt he registered the mental reflection that that certainly *was* the much talked of 'hot stuff.'" Since skeptics in the group insisted the toad would die, the engineer had him put in a wooden box and shut up overnight. The Old Doctor concludes his story with a comic snapper. "As I live, boys, next morning that toad was not only alive, but gave unmistakable evidence of being hungry! He recognized the major and winked at him; and when a candle-bug . . . was thrown in the box, the frog snapped him up like a trout would a minnow; fact" (113–17).

The humor of the Southern foot-soldier—at least it was humorous in retrospect—became legendary. Daniel remembered a fat young fellow of about twenty-two, who, pretending concern over an older man in the company, approached the drill sergeant after a double-timing exercise and, gasping for breath, suggested: "Sergeant—I wouldn't—make—the—men double-quick up the hill; it tires Mr. Russell so bad." Mr. Russell, about fifty, was seated on a log gently fanning himself (22–24).

The company wit was always the most popular man in the outfit. Writers of war memoirs seldom had trouble remembering him. In *Co. Aytch* Sam Watkins painted the following character sketch:

> A big strapping fellow by the name of Tennessee Thompson always carried bigger burdens than any other five men in the army. For example, he carried two quilts, three blankets, one gum oil cloth, one overcoat, one axe, one hatchet, one camp-kettle, one oven and lid, one coffee pot, besides his knapsack, haversack, canteen, gun, cartridge-box, and three days' rations. He was a rare bird, anyhow. Tennessee usually had his hair cut short on one side and left long on the other, so that he could give his head a bow and a toss and throw the long hairs over on the other side, and it would naturally part itself without a comb. Tennessee was the wit and good nature of the company; always in a good humor, and ever ready to do any duty when called upon. In fact, I would sometimes get out of heart and low spirited, and would hunt up Tennessee to have a little fun. His bye-word was "Bully for Bragg; he's hell on retreat, and will whip the Yankees yet" (97).

Even the preachers could play the humorist. Daniel told of an Episcopal minister, who was also captain of the company, whose custom it was to hold frequent prayer meetings for his men. He suddenly, however, stopped these meetings with the explanation that "he had been fighting the devil all his life, and now that he had the Yankees to fight in addition, doubling on him as it were, he couldn't do justice to both" (46–47).

Watkins pokes gentle fun at his company chaplain, a learned divine from Nashville who began his first service with a prayer which sounded to Watkins like "O, Thou immaculate, invisible, eternal and holy Being, the exudations of whose effulgence illuminate this terrestrial sphere, we approach Thy presence, being covered all over with wounds and bruises and putrifying sores, from the crowns of our heads to the soles of our feet. And Thou, O Lord, art our dernier resort." The prayer continues in this tone of polysyllabic profundity *ad infinitum* and leads Watkins to comment: "In fact, he was so 'high larnt' that I don't think anyone understood him but the generals." The minister finally began to preach a roaring war sermon, damning the Yankees, saying they should be fought in this world and their ghosts chased into the next. And then, in Watkins's words, "About this time we heard the awfullest racket, produced by some wild animal tearing through the woods towards us, and the cry, 'Look out! look out! hooie! hooie! look out!' and there came running right through our midst a wild bull, mad with terror and fright, running right over and knocking down the divine, and scattering Bibles and hymn books in every direction. The services were brought to a close without the doxology." During the attack at Chickamauga the same chaplain was riding along inciting the men on. With shells screaming through the air, he was saying: "Remember, boys, that he who is killed will sup tonight in Paradise." Then a loud soldier shouted to him, "Well, parson, you come along and take supper with us." Suddenly a bomb burst near the preacher and he put spurs to his horse and was next seen advancing to the rear, with almost every soldier yelling "The parson isn't hungry, and never eats supper" (113–14). But all this taunting was good-natured; chaplains were generally held in high esteem among the men.

IN *A REBEL'S RECOLLECTIONS* Eggleston sketched some odd characters he knew in the Southern army, characters like Jack Hawkins, one of "our assortment of queer people," who was inoffensive and timid but who sang "bold robber songs in the metallic voice peculiar to vocalists of the circus." He recalled old Denton, who would describe sumptuous imaginary feasts on an empty stomach. "'You ought to have dined with me today,' he would say. 'I had a deviled leg of turkey, and some beautiful broiled oysters with spanish olives. I never eat broiled oysters without olives. You try it sometime, and you'll never regret it. Then I had a stuffed wild goose's liver. Did you ever eat one? Well, you don't know what a real tidbit is, then. Not stuffed in the ordinary way, but stuffed scientifically and cooked in a way you never saw it done before.'" Eggleston also remembers "the most ingenious malingerer I ever heard of" who "was never off the sick-list for a single day." He was completely inured to "the gibes of the men, the sneers of the surgeons, and the denunciations of the officers." After being dismissed from one hospital he would start toward his unit "and continue in that direction till he came to another infirmary, when he would have a relapse at once, and gain admission there." The doctors used all manner of remedies to get rid of him. "They burned his back with hot coppers; gave him the most nauseous mixture; put him on the lowest possible diet; treated him to cold shower-baths four or five times daily . . . but all to no purpose." Only the end of the war relieved them of him (186–91).

The camp storyteller, "big, strong, jolly" Bill Hicks, remained a pleasant and poignant memory for F. E. Daniel. Once, the Old Doctor recalls, Bill told of a dogfight, realistically "imitating the big dog how *he* 'went,' and the little dog how *he* 'went.'" After he had told several times how the big dog would jump at the little dog and go "gh-r-r-rh" and how the little dog would catch the big dog by the leg and go "br-e-w-r-r-rer," Tump Dixon, a bully from an adjoining camp, came up and insisted he tell the story again. When Bill refused, the bully pulled out a six-shooter and leveled it at his head and said: "How-did-that-big-dog-go?"—and Bill showed him. Then he said: "How-did-that-little-dog-go?"—and

Bill showed him again. The performance was repeated until the boys were yelling with laughter and Bill got mad. The Old Doctor concludes, "Tump left presently, and any time after that, if one wanted to get a fight on his hands he had only to ask Bill 'how the big dog went?'" (30–33).

Other sketches of Bill include the time several men found him sleeping soundly under a tree, tied up his jaws, crossed his hands on his breast, and had begun his burial service when the "corpse" was awakened by a call to report to the captain's tent. But Bill did not allow his "undertakers" to go unpunished. Another time when the author and Bill fell out of ranks to pick blackberries, they heard strange voices. Trying to hide, Bill plumped down into a bumblebee's nest. Daniel's recollection of the scene is semi-sadistic. "He ran again—you bet he did! and such a sight I never saw—Bill running like a scared deer, and fighting those bumblebees off with both hands, and every now and then, as one would get in his work, to hear Bill yell was just too funny for anything in this world, unless it be a Wild-west show" (37). This sketch shows that, even with the postwar trend toward a less painful, less sadistic humor, discomfiture was still the source of much mirth. Immediately following these incidents, however, Daniel returned to the more typical mood of his time. The lines drip with sentiment and pathos: "Alas, poor Bill! He was a fine young man, an Apollo in form, and a model of strong physical manhood. Had he lived he would surely have had a career of usefulness. But like thousands of others of the flower of the youth of the South he was needlessly sacrificed to what the South believed to be principle" (43–44). The war had made a difference.

The author of *Detailed Minutiae of Soldier Life* sketched in humorous caricature the military types he found in his company. These types include the "General" of the mess, who knows all about forthcoming campaigns—with details; "the Bore" or "the Old Auger," who begins to tell a story and takes hours to get to the point;

"the Singing Man," who sings the men to sleep with "Virginia, Virginia, the Land of the Free" and "Dixie"; "the Recruit," with "his nice new clothes, new hat, new knife for all the fellows to borrow, nice comb for general use, nice little glass to shave by, good smoking tobacco, money in his pocket to lend out . . ."; "the Scribe," who could write a two-hour pass and sign the captain's name better than the captain himself; "the Mischievous Man," who would volunteer to shave a man with a big beard and moustache with his own razor, but would walk off after shaving half his face; "the Forager," who could tell "if there was buttermilk anywhere inside of ten miles" and who would get the spareribs if anybody in the country was killing a hog; "the Commissary Man," who never had any sugar over, or any salt or soda or coffee; "the Honest Man," "who would not eat stolen pig," but would "take a little of the gravy." In addition, McCarthy lists "the Bully," "the Argument Man," "the Lazy Man," and "the Worthless Man" (200–210). Most of these types were exploited in postwar Southern humor.

NOTES

1. *Sidney Lanier: A Biographical and Critical Study* (Chapel Hill, 1933), 106.
2. *Ibid.*, 50.
3. Alexander E. Sweet and J. Armory Knox, *On a Mexican Mustang through Texas, from the Gulf to the Rio Grande* (Hartford, 1883) ; these two men in 1881 founded the humor magazine *Texas Siftings* in Austin; in 1885 it was moved to New York, where it folded in 1897.
4. *Co. Aytch, Maury Grays, First Tennessee Regiment;* or, *A Side Show of the Big Show* (Nashville, 1882).
5. Wiley's *The Life of Johnny Reb* (Indianapolis, 1943) is an excellent study of the common soldier of the Confederacy. Wiley has also edited Lt. William N. Woods's *Reminiscences of Big I* (Jackson, Tenn., 1956), the Virginian's memoirs of his experiences as a Confederate officer. The recollections are not primarily humorous but contain humorous incidents such as "The Cat Wouldn't Cook Done," in which Wood relates that a cat was still too tough to eat after two days' boiling.
6. In his *Rebel Private* (17–18), William A. Fletcher also touched on the ubiquitous louse. This was the procedure, he recalled, for delousing an affected

pair of pants or a shirt: "Our plan was, when they got so thick that they were hardly bearable, to make a fire of a small amount of straw or leaves and hold the garment over the blaze and from the heat they would drop off, be burned, or be ready for the next fellow. If one was well stocked with big fat fellows, it would remind him of popping corn. The uneducated may think I have said too much for truth of this subject; but if he or she will ask some old 'battle-scarred soldier' he will give you a few lines more."

7. W. C. King and W. P. Derby (eds.), *Camp-Fire Sketches and Battlefield Echoes of the Rebellion* (Springfield, Mass., 1887), 554.
8. *The Grayjackets and How They Lived, Fought and Died, for Dixie* . . . by a Confederate (Richmond, 1867), 139–40; reprinted in *A Treasury of Southern Folklore*, 12.
9. Eggleston, *A Rebel's Recollections*, 155–56.
10. *Camp-Fire Sketches*, 563.
11. *Co. Aytch*, 60.
12. William Jones, *Personal Reminiscences, Anecdotes and Letters of General Robert E. Lee* (New York, 1876) 242–44; reprinted in *A Treasury of Southern Folklore*, 175–76.
13. *Camp-Fire Sketches*, 563–64.
14. *War Years with Jeb Stuart*, 174.
15. *A Rebel's Recollections*, 126–27.

3

The Negroes

Negroes contributed more to the war than merely keeping their masters' clothes clean and entertaining them with anthropomorphic stories of their religion. The Aunt Daphnes and the Uncle Zacks did their part, but it was a small one. A far more important role was played by the Negro valet who accompanied his owner to the war and remained with him until the war ended—or one of them was killed. Many are the stories of Negroes who fought heroically to protect their masters. Armistead Churchill Gordon's "Envion" is about just such a faithful slave, who fought by the side of his master until the master was killed. Envion then buried him on the battlefield and went home to tell his mistress the sad news. His conduct in the war is his consolation in old age. He soliloquizes: "I ain't nothin' but a poor good-for-nothin' nigger; but it does me some good ter remember dat I fit in de battle 'long side o' de braves' man dat was in dat wah; an' dat when I come back I tuk keer o' young Miss Agnes."[1] This selection by Gordon sets the pattern for most postwar pictures of the Negro in the war: faithful, comic, and scornful of the invaders. The Negro who escaped into the Federal armies and freedom is seldom treated.

In Harry Stillwell Edwards's "Captain Isam" a Negro bodyguard decides to help in the actual fighting and gets the regimental colonel's permission to organize the other Negro valets into a fighting unit.[2] What happens is a farce. Justifying his petition to the colonel, he says, "You see, Mas' Alec, hyah ez thirty-two niggers waitin' on folks in dis hyah camp, holdin' hosses, cleanin' brasses, an' cookin'; an' hit don' look right fer dese lazy rascals ter be er-settin' roun' while fightin' 's goin' on, an' dey bosses out yonner somewhar, reskin' dey lives ter keep' 'em fum bein' stole an' runned off by dem Yankees" (182).

After permission is granted, Isam keeps his dusky troops drilling for hours each day in preparation for their first battle. He also decides he'd better get the rules of warfare straight before his initiation and asks a white officer, "Boss, when we gets dere an' goes ter fightin', ez hit 'g'inst de rules ter tek res' an' shoot? Some er dese niggers can't hit er mount'in ercross er hog-pen 'lessen dey teks res'. Ef dey can't tek res', 'spec' er heap er Gen'l Bragg's powdah an' shot be wasted right dere dis mornin'" (186). As zero hour approaches, Isam begins lining his men up for the charge and giving them orders: "Berry Bowles ez de bigges' an' de fus' man in de line, an' he mus' lead de way an' y'-all des foller right erlong en es tracks. Berry, you mek fer dat pine ovah yonner on de ridge, an' I'm comin' 'long berhin' de las' man; an' de fus' nigger what bre'k ranks ez got me ter run ovah 'fo' he leave. I done gi' y'-all fair warnin'; an' ef anybody git dis sword stuck frough 'im, ain' my funer'l march!" (187).

They are about to leave when a cannon blows up a short distance away and the Negroes scatter. They begin praying and soon a mighty revival is in progress, complete with spirituals. The Negro platoon advances only at the command of a white officer with a pistol in his hand. Their conduct under fire, however, was not very exemplary. Isam later explains that as they were advancing a cannon ball landed nearby and the Negroes scattered: "Dey runned ober me, an' 'fo' I knowed what my name was, de groun' was full er guns an' tracks. I got on top er stump an' hollered loud ez I could holler, an', 'fo' Gord, de onliest nigger en sight was Berry, what done fell over er log, an' was des layin' dere prayin' fer somebody ter tell es Mas' George ter sen' de doctor quick. I knowed dere warn' no use er my stan'in' up dere fer fo' thousan' Yankees ter be shootin' at, an' I got down an' went 'long back, sorter singin' ter merse'f ter let folks know I warn' anxious ter leave" (190–91). When he gets back to safe ground where the other Negroes are, he begins rationalizing their behavior and the need for him to stay behind the lines: "An' den hit come ter me dat ev'y nigger dere was worf er thousan' dollahs, an' some er dey marsters was po' white men, an' couldn' 'ford ter lose er nigger. So I said I reck'n Gen'l Bragg an' Mas' Alec done look atter dat little bunch er Yankees out en front, an' I better stay back dere an' keep dem niggers an' waggins fum bein' runned off" (191). Thus bravely standing guard duty behind the lines, Isam figures he saved the Confederacy $32,000 worth of Negroes and a wagon train at Chickamauga.[3]

Uncle Remus, however, is better able to adapt to the demands of war than Isam. His is a much more serious contribution, too. Although he remains behind to protect his white women, he briefly enters the war to save the life of his beloved master. Joel Chandler Harris records this adventure of Uncle Remus in "A Story of the War."[4] In the sketch the old Negro tells Miss Theodosia Huntingdon, his employer's sister down from Vermont, of his war experiences. When the war first started, he says, "hit didn't strike me dat dey wuz enny war gwine on, en ef I hadn't sorter miss de nabers, en seed fokes gwine outer de way fer ter ax de news, I'd a 'lowed ter myse'f dat de war wuz 'way off 'mong some yuther country." Soon, however, the war came closer; and when all the white men were gone from the place, his "ole Miss" sent for him and said, "Remus, I ain't got nobody fer ter look arter the place but you." Pledging that his mistress could "des 'pen' on de ole nigger," he says he took over the plantation "en you better b'leeve I bossed dem han's." Sounding like his white master, he says he worked the Negroes hard, but adds, "But dey wuz tuk keer un. Dey had plenty er cloze en plenty er grub, en dey wuz de fattes' niggers in de settlement" (123–24).

He then proudly explains how he defended the plantation when the Yankees came. After hiding the cattle, horses, grain, and hogs, he says, "I put on my Sunday cloze en groun' my axe. Two whole days I groun' dat axe. De grinestone wuz in sight er de gate en close ter de big 'ouse, en dar I tuck my stan'" (124). When the Yanks came they ransacked the place, but Uncle Remus took up a protective vigil near Ole Miss and Miss Sally. After the Federals left he took his gun to go see about the stock, but on the way he spied a Yankee sniper firing from a tree. As Remus watched, he suddenly saw his master riding down the road toward the sniper. He recalls his quick action. "I know'd dat man wuz gwineter shoot Mars Jeems ef he could, en dat wuz mo'n I could stan'. Manys en manys de time dat I nuss dat boy, en hilt 'im in dese arms, en toted 'im on dis back, en w'en I see dat Yankee lay dat gun 'cross a lim' en take aim at Mars Jeems I up wid my ole rifle, en shet my eyes en let de man have all she had" (126). As Remus finishes this part of his story, his Northern auditor asks indignantly: "Do you mean to say that you shot the Union soldier, when you knew he was fighting for your freedom?" But Uncle Remus is ready for her question and answers, "Co'se, I know all about dat, en it sorter made cole chills run up my back; but w'en I see dat man take aim, en Mars Jeems gwine home ter Ole Miss en Miss Sally, I des disremembered all 'bout freedom en lammed aloose" (126). The wounded soldier was cared for, the old Negro adds, by Miss Sally; and pointing to Miss Theodosia's brother, says "en now dar he is." Like almost all of Harris's work dealing with the war, this story shows how the war eventually united the nation more strongly than ever.[5] The symbol of this union is the marriage of a Northern man and a Southern woman.

Like Uncle Remus, the slaves left behind on the plantation are usually accorded the responsibility—at least in fictional humor—of "protecting" or "looking after" the women. In addition, they break bad news of a loved one's death to the mistress,[6] they take her to see a wounded son or husband,[7] and they constantly worry about the safety of their masters fighting far away from home. Jeannette Walworth's picture of a doting mammy was duplicated many times in humorous sketches: "What a despot she was! What a gentle, tart, coaxable, domineering old paradox, whom we children loved and feared extravagantly and unreasonably." When her master's son left for the war, she gave him a black quart bottle filled with her special preparation and said, "H'it's balsam apple and whisky. It's might good for cuts en bruises, en ef my chillun git hurt, Mammy won' be nigh 'em to ten' 'em lak she wants t' be, but you jes' rub dat balsam apple inter de place right quick en h'it mebbe be de savin' ub yo' libes, son. If you git out'n it, write to Mammy for some mo'." Thus Mammy figures that, in a sense, she can accompany her young master to the battlefield.[8]

One of the infrequent treatments of the unfaithful Negro, however, is found in this same sketch. Mammy's husband deserts to Vicksburg, where he believes he will get "a guv'ment mule en ten acres er groun' by goin' arter it." Mammy is depressed by her husband's absence, and when her son leaves, too, she cannot stand her lonesome cabin any longer and reluctantly follows them. Unable to stay away from her white people, however, she returns after the war to help them "reconstruct" their lives.

ON THE OTHER HAND, John T. Moore's stories of Negroes and the war are solidly and consistently in the faithful darky tradition. Paralleling the sentiments of H. S. Edwards's Isam are those of Moore's Dick. Hearing the noise of a battle being fought near his master's plantation, Dick asks indignantly, "Whut dese Yankees wanter cum down heah an' take our niggers 'way frum us fur ennyway? Whut we done to dem? All we ax 'em ter do is ter let us erlone." In this war sketch, "Dick," Moore becomes polemical, writing in such defensive passages as the following: "Where Dick got the sentiments he expressed I cannot say; but I do know that Dick was no exception to his race. Darkey like, he was for his home and his white people first, though the freedom of all his race lay on the other side." Seldom was a Southerner so explicit in his defense of "the peculiar institution" of the South. "Some day there is going to be a great monument put up in the South by the southern people. And on its top is going to be a negro—not the mythical slave with chains on him and terror in his face, which fool artists, who never saw a negro slave, and fool poets, who never heard one laugh, are wont to depict—but the jolly, contented, rollicking rascal that we knew and loved; the member of our household and sharer of our joys and sorrows. On its top, I say, there is going to be that kind of negro, as he was, and he is going to be represented in the act of picking cotton, with a laugh, while he refuses with scorn a gun with which to fight his master for his own freedom. When that is done, it will be the crowning monument of the age."[9] Into these words Moore condensed a popular Southern—and national—attitude toward the Negro slave in the postwar period. Using this attitude as a hypothesis, Southern humorists filled their writings with contented slaves.

The most devoted war Negroes of the lot are, naturally, those delineated by the arch-apologist for the South, Thomas Nelson Page. His Uncle Balla is the epitome of the faithful slave during the war. When his mistress tells him that he is free to leave, he answers her with a puzzled question: "Hi, Mistis . . . whar is I got to go? I wuz born on dis place an' I 'spec' to die here, an' be buried right *yonder*" and he points toward the graveyard and continues with a pledge, "Y'all sticks by us, and we'll stick by you."[10] Uncle Balla knew that the future was to be a trying time for both white and black Southerners and that in union there was strength.

The Negro's unenthusiastic reaction to freedom was often depicted comically. In Opie Read's "An Ivory Smile," said to be based on fact, a Kentucky planter before the war decides to make his favorite slave, Amos, a present of his freedom for Christmas. The owner recalls the scene in which he first said:

> "Amos, I am going to give you something which many of the world's greatest men have died for, and for which any great man would shed his blood. Amos, I give you freedom."
>
> He did not bound into the air, as I had expected; he wiped his mouth with the back of his hand, and quietly said: "I 'lowed you gwine gimme dat 'possum dog."
>
> "What! You old rascal," I exclaimed, "would you rather have a dog than your freedom?"
>
> He looked up and thus replied: "Er ole man kin hab comfort wid er 'possum dog, sah, but when freedom comes ter er ole man it makes him feel foolish."

Unlike most fictional Negroes, however, Amos made the most of his freedom; and during the war he saved his former owner's life and told him that at last he had forgiven him "fur not makin' me er present o' dat 'possum dog."[11] To most postwar humorists the "good" Negro refused to exercise his new freedom during the war. Even if he left to seek "a guv'ment mule en ten acres er groun'," he returned before long with an empty stomach and a begging mouth.

NOTES

1. *Library of Southern Literature*, V, 1906.
2. *His Defense and Other Stories* (New York, 1922), 181–92.
3. A different version of the Negro's conduct under fire is found in Thomas Wentworth Higginson, *Army Life in a Black Regiment* (Boston, 1870). Higginson's view of the Negro is admittedly biased, but he had occasion as colonel in command of the first African American regiment mustered during the war, the First South Carolina Volunteers, to observe the Negro.
4. *Uncle Remus: His Songs and His Sayings* (New York, 1957), 121–26.
5. An earlier version of the same story, published in the *Atlanta Constitution*,

October 14, 1877, is much more realistic and not nearly so conciliatory. Entitled "Uncle Remus as a Rebel," the story has Uncle Remus kill the Yankee sniper. "We had ter cut down der tree fer ter bury 'im."

6. See Sherwood Bonner, "Gran'mammy," *Suwanee River Tales* (1884).
7. See Jeanne'te Walworth, *Uncle Scipio* (1896).
8. *Southern Silhouettes* (New York, 1887). 133, 138.
9. *Ole Mistis and Other Songs and Stories from Tennessee* (Nashville, 1925), 124.
10. *Two Little Confederates* (New York, 1888), 49–50.
11. *Odd Folks* (New York, 1897), 127, 132.

4

The Poor Whites

Although Union sentiment was strong among poor whites in east Tennessee, southwest Virginia, northwest North Carolina, north Alabama and Mississippi, and western Georgia, the poor white generally aligned himself with the slaveowner to present a united front when the war came.[1] Historians have posited many explanations for the phenomenon of the poor white fighting "the rich man's war": he was harangued by secessionist orators like William L. Yancey, he didn't like the thought of equality and competition with the Negro, and he did like excitement. Once in the army he was usually a good fighter—he had been shooting rabbits and squirrels since he was big enough to hold a gun in his hands—but he couldn't abide the strict military discipline and desertion was very common. More likely than not, he had a good reason for deserting: his family was starving; consequently the deserter is most often presented sympathetically in postwar humor. In Harris's *On the Plantation,* a man who deserted to return to his starving family defines a deserter as one of "these here fellers what jines inter the army an' then comes home arter awhile without lief or license."[2] Harris also treated the deserter in "At Teague Poteet's," in which he pictured Georgia crackers dodging Confederate conscript officers and usually outwitting them.

An Alabama cracker who is a deserter is the subject of Samuel Mintern Peck's "Far from the Front."[3] The Alabama local colorist notes the waning of enthusiasm for the war among the poor whites living in the hills of west Alabama. In biblical style Peck wrote of the hard times the poor women were having: "And it came to pass that many of the wives of the poor non-slaveowning whites who dwelt in the hills sometimes asked themselves if they were not paying too dearly for the possibility of some day owning a negro, and other benefits promised by secession" (285). This sketch is about a man who deserts to his starving wife and children about the time the war ends. Because Lee surrendered before his absence was found out, no one ever knew of his desertion except his wife.

Another story by Peck, "Pap's Mules," tells how a cracker family's mules were saved from Yankee soldiers by the heroism of one small boy (91–123). The poor Cline family was living life about the same as always, when the widow Barbour, who delighted in terrifying people with her gossip of imminent Yankee raids, came by to warn them and to chastise them for going about life as usual. "The day o' wrath's at han', Susan Cline . . . an' you pore critters are washin' clo'es, churnin' milk, an' bilin' soap!" Having just come from Oakville, the nearby village, she describes for the Clines the ludicrous preparations being made there for defending the town. The villagers are not deluded into thinking they can successfully keep back the enemy, but to surrender the town without even a token struggle would be unthinkable and dishonorable. The Clines don't appear to be upset by the widow's bad tidings; but that night their small boy saves their mules by taking them into the swamp in case the Yankees should come by.

Meanwhile Oakville is preparing for her heroic but futile defense. The mayor's patriotism reaches its high-water mark. "The old mayor was . . . proud. What was a war governor beside a raid mayor! To repulse the enemy had been beyond his expectation; and when it was discovered at daylight that they were fifteen hundred strong, while the Home Guard were but fifty, his honor remarked to a friend that no braver defense was recorded in the pages of history" (106).

After the raid is over and the Yankees leave, Widow Barbour conducts a survey of the damage done, hoping to find a lot; but she is especially disappointed to find little touched at the Clines'. "'The fence is all thar and the beegums is standin'. Nothin's tore down,' she sighed, regretfully. 'Howsomever, I don't hear no hens cacklin',' and her eyes brightened. 'But thar's the old black sow sunnin' herself agin the fence fat as ever,' she added sorrowfully" (119–20). To her dismay she even finds the Clines' mule safe. She could glean no bad news at the Clines' to spread around the community. In fact, while she's there John Cline returns from Oakville with startling information. "Word's come that Lee's surrendered, and the war's done." Many another suffering poor white considered that good news.

AN INCIDENT IN SIDNEY Lanier's war novel shows the widespread discontent among poor whites with the war. A Tennessee deserter's family is more concerned about what the neighbors will say than about the service he could have rendered the Confederacy had he stayed with the army. His brother gives him a tongue-lashing: "Hit don't make much diff'ence to me now, whether we whips the Yanks or they whips us. What good'll it do ef we do conquer 'em? Everybody'll be a-shoutin' an' a-hurrahin' an' they'll leave *us* out of the frolic, for we is kin to a deserter! An' the women'll be a-smilin' on them that has lived to git home, one minute, an' the next they'll be a-weepin' for them that's left dead in Virginny an' Pennsylvany an' Tennessy—but *you* won't git home, an' *you* won't be left dead nowher; they cain't neither smile at you nor cry for you; what'll they do ef anybody speaks yer name? Gore Smallin, they'll lift their heads high an' we'll hang our'n low. They'll scorn ye an' we'll blush for ye."[4] If this reaction is typical, family shame for deserters was common all over the South; but contrary to Lanier, desertion doesn't seem to have been much of a family stigma among poor whites.

In the humorous sketch by John Fox Jr., "The Army of the Callahan," the author relates how the proprietor of a crossroads store in western Virginia tried to get protection against Union raiders from Kentucky.[5] When the storekeeper heard that raiders were coming to destroy the property of Confederate sympathizers in the settlement, he pulled a hoax designed to save his property. He forged an order from Jefferson Davis to a gullible and vain old man in the community commanding him to muster a home guard to protect the property of the Confederate citizens. The plan almost backfires when the commander of the guard appoints the merchant commissary general with the duty of supplying the home-guard army of freeloaders with rations. The property of the Rebels is not harmed when the raiders come through, but not because the home guard defended it, for the men broke ranks and fled in fear when the enemy first appeared.

Although Thomas Nelson Page concentrated on the effect of the war on the slavocracy in *Two Little Confederates*, he touched on the poor whites at the periphery of plantation life (31 ff). Describing the poor whites who lived in the community known as Holetown, he wrote: "They were inoffensive people, and their worst vices were intemperance and evasion of the tax-laws." At the outbreak of the war most of the eligible men in Holetown enlisted in the Confederate service, but many soon tired of army discipline and returned to care for their poverty-stricken families; consequently Holetown was a favorite hunting ground for deserters. The two little Confederates have many amusing adventures hunting deserters in the community, and they once capture a member of the conscript guard. The poor-white women warn their menfolk of deserter hunters by blowing on a horn; they called it "jes' blowin' fur Millindy to come to dinner," but there must have been many Millindys because horns sounded all through the settlement when soldiers were near.

Many poor-white men took the war casually. When they fought, they fought like the devil, but when they got tired of it they went home. Sometimes they returned to fight again. In *Two Little Confederates* Page recorded the defiant words of a returned soldier to his commander: "Cun'l . . . I ain't no deserter. I ain't feared of bein' shot. Ef I was, I wouldn' 'a' come here now. I'm gwine wid you, an' I'm gwine back to my company; an' I'm gwine fight, ef Yankees gits in my way; but ef I gits tired, I's comin' home; an' tain't no use to tell you I ain't, 'cause I *is*,—an' ef anybody flings up to me that I's a-runnin' away, I'm gwine to kill 'em!" (114). Knowing the man will make good his pledge and threat, the colonel agrees to his terms.

Not all poor whites took the war so lightly. In "The Bushwhackers" Charles Egbert Craddock told the story of a young mountaineer in Unionist east Tennessee who proudly fought in the Confederate army.[6] To his mother's complaint that he was too young to enlist, he threatened: "I'll jes' set an' spin like a sure-enough gal ef ye won't let me go an' jine the army like a boy" (11). One day a Rebel company camped nearby and he joined it. Saying goodby to his girl, he proudly announced: "An' I ain't no hand ter dodge bullets, nuther" (32). In his company he was nicknamed Baby Bunting because of his youth and became popular with all the men, who often made him the butt of their good-humored pranks. The only cruelty in the sketch was the beating of Baby Bunting by one of his own cowardly comrades, which caused him to lose an arm. The Yanks were always mentioned favorably.

While her son was fighting for the Confederacy, the mother at home lamented his decision to join the Rebel side. She told a neighbor, "Ye know I war fur the Union, an' so war his dad. . . . My old man had been ailin' ennyhows, but this hyar talk o' bustin' up the Union—why, it jes' fairly harried him inter his grave. An' I 'lowed ez Hil'ry would be fur the Union, too, like everybody in the mountings ez hed good sense. But when a critter-company o'

Confeds rid up the mounting one day Hil'ry he talk with some of 'em, an' he was war stubborn ever after. An' so he jined the critter company" (78–79).

After his arm was amputated, Hilary returned home, where he found everyone frightened by bushwhackers, who were threatening the area. The boy's mother lent a note of unconscious humor to the tense situation when she said, "It air powerful selfish, I know, ter hope the bushwhackers'll forage on somebody else's poultry an' sech, but somehows my own chickens seem nigher kin ter me than other folkses' be. I never seen no sech ten-toed chickens ez mine nowhar" (90–91). The men of the neighborhood, however, banded together and fought off the bushwhackers when they attacked. Like so much postwar fiction, the story ends on a note of religious sentiment. Men who had been through the hell of war supposedly had had a foretaste of the real hell and wanted to avoid going there.

In 1871 Dr. George W. Bagby, under the nom de plume of Mozis Addums, published a poor white's "Histry uv the Waw" in *The Southern Magazine.*[7] Although the work is a masterpiece of irony, Mozis maintained in the "Introducktory" that his only objective was to write for money. His history would be a departure from the usual. "Far frum imitating the exampul of the Waw Department at Washintun, and tellin uv the truth recklissly and regardliss of konsekenses, I shall not hesitate, whenever it suit my puppus, to tell the most infunnul lies that ever issued frum mortul man. . . . I make out my kase in my oan mind befo startin, and then wuk the facts up to it." His history, he continued, would be partial to the South "be-caws I don't know ennything about the other side (altho' I've red thar ofishul repotes, and thar still mo reliabul newspapers) and don't want to know nuthin 'bout it." The book would also be "the only trewly vallibul historrikul Wuk which has apeard since the Book uv Jobe—which he was a good histoarianer, becaws he confined himself to a narrytiv uv his oan suffrins, with a okashunal excurshun discriptiv uv wild asses, waw-hosses, and the hevinly boddies." By offending as many people as he could he thought his history would gain notoriety and thus a large sale. He concluded his introduction: "The world is full of corns, made to be trod on, espeshly by histoarians uv thar own times; and I be durn ef I dont inten to tred on as menny uv 'em as I possibly kin. But Confedrit corns, I shell tred litely on um." Mozis' history of the war, therefore, is written exclusively from a Southern viewpoint.

NOTES

1. Clifford Dowdey, *Experiment in Rebellion* (New York, 1946), 379–80.
2. *On the Plantation: A Story of a Georgia Boy's Adventures During the War* (New York, 1892), 138.
3. *Alabama Sketches* (Chicago, 1902), 285–99.
4. *Tiger-Lilies* (New York, 1867), 155.
5. *Christmas Eve on Lonesome* (New York, 1904), 17–73.
6. *The Bushwhackers and Other Stories* (Chicago, 1899), 3–115.
7. VIII (Jan., 1871), 70–72; the "Histry" was continued through the year.

5

The Folks at Home

The noncombatants during the Civil War frequently suffered as much as the soldiers. The women, the children, and the aged left behind were often without protection and adequate supplies. What food they had was subject to be commandeered by foraging soldiers of both sides. To keep family valuables safe they had to be buried and livestock had to be hidden in swamps, and sometimes even these precautions were not effective. After enemy troops passed through with their flaming torches, many families did not even have a house to sleep in. In spite of deprivation and separation from loved ones suffered by those unable to fight, however, postwar humorists could still find subject matter in the folks that stayed behind.

If memoirs of prison life were usually grim, a few were amusing. During the war Jane Tandy Cross was imprisoned for her Southern sentiments. Out of her experiences she wrote a series of amusing and pathetic letters dealing with prison life which she published as *Six Months Under a Cloud.* The Virginian Sara Agnes Pryor recorded her Civil War experiences in *Reminiscences of Peace and War* (1904), her most popular book. An indication of the book's humor is Ellen Glasgow's mention of it in a letter to a friend: "Last night I sat up spellbound until I finished it, beginning with laughter and ending in real tears. . . . The tragedy of it I can understand, for it is not difficult to be tragic—but the delicious, piquant, never-failing humor—the humor that brightens tears, this, I confess, has taken me completely captive."[1] Women writers and women readers did much to promote the vogue of such crying humor in the postwar South.

One of the most popular of the Southern writers, Thomas Nelson Page wrote many stories set during the war; but none has been more frequently read and enjoyed than *Two Little Confederates*. This book is an entertaining account of boys' life on a Virginia plantation during the war. The patriotic fervor of the little Rebels, Frank and Willy, leads them to organize drills using wooden guns made for them by Uncle Balla, the faithful old Negro driver. A dozen or so little Negroes fill in the ranks. Their exciting war adventures include catching a Rebel soldier raiding their hen house and being caught by Yankee soldiers. One of their not unusual pastimes was observing battles fought near their home. One day, while they were watching a battle and were a little too close to the front, bullets got to flying near them and the little colored boys with them:

> "What's them things 'zip-zippin' 'round my ears?" asked one of the negro boys.
>
> "Bullets," said Frank, proud of his knowledge.
>
> "Will they hurt me if they hit me?"
>
> "Of course they will. They'll kill you."
>
> "I'm gwine home," said the boy, and off he started with a trot (133).

Harris's *On the Plantation: A Story of a Georgia Boy's Adventures During the War* is based at least partly on the author's wartime experiences as a printer's devil on the Joseph Addison Turner plantation in middle Georgia. Most of the humor in the novel comes from Joe Maxwell, the "Georgia boy," who was full of pranks and tricks and had a reputation for humor. The main business of the book is to show plantation life—often austere, dangerous, and tragic but also exciting, humorous, and rewarding—along the route of

Sherman's march to the sea.

Samuel M. Peck's local stories of the Civil War have a gentle humor and an absence of the sectional bitterness characteristic of Southern humor written after Reconstruction. Two of the stories in his *Alabama Sketches* are set on the home front—"The Maid of Jasmindale" and "Under the White Rose-Tree." The first is the love story of a returning Confederate soldier who visits an Alabama friend and falls in love with his sister (171–91). The young couple's romance goes smoothly until the Alabama belle overhears her lover and her brother laughing and talking about Katie, and assuming this to be her lover's Kentucky girl, she shuns him and becomes incommunicado when he's around. When the Kentuckian discovers the cause of her strange behavior, he puts their romance back on course by laughingly explaining: "Why—Katie is the name of a cannon in our battery. The boys used to name the guns for their sweethearts. I named my gun Katie because I was ashamed to confess I had no sweetheart." He seals their reconciliation by chiding, "And you were jealous of a gun!"

The plot of "Under the White Rose-Tree" is concerned with how a middle-aged bachelor is made to realize his love for a next-door spinster by the exigencies of war (219–38). Miss Melinda entrusts Professor Winston with her grandmother's gold thimble to bury just before the Yankees raid the town. After elaborate preparations he finally decides on putting the thimble and his prize watch in a tobacco box and burying it under his rose tree. The Yankee raiders come and one is billeted on the professor's front porch. The first night after the professor buries the treasure he has a nightmare: he dreams that his watch is talking to him and reminding him that it hasn't been wound. The watch is in danger of running down—something that hasn't happened in thirty-five years! Awaking from his bad dream, the professor steals from the house, digs up the box, winds the watch, and replaces it in its cache. While he is doing this he is being watched by the good-for-nothing son of his colored cook, who quickly goes to the hiding place to steal the treasure. Another person, however, has also been watching the nocturnal prowling, the Yankee sentinel bedded on the front porch; and he intercepts the Negro boy and returns the box to the professor before he leaves the next day. This little serio-comic episode makes the professor and his neighbor aware of their affection for each other. The sketch contains no hint of bitterness against the Union troops. The hero of the story, in fact, is the Yankee soldier who saves the professor's watch and his ladyfriend's thimble.

AS UNLIKELY AS IT may seem, humor thus played a significant part in the bloody epic that was the American Civil War. It was humor which helped to keep the South fighting against insurmountable odds for four years. In the face of hunger, inadequate clothing and supplies, and superior numbers, the Southern soldier was sustained by his sense of humor. W. W. Blackford testified:

> War develops an infinite amount of wit and humor among soldiers. In every company there were aspirants for the honor of being the 'funny man' of the command, whose study it was to get off good jokes; and between the companies of a regiment there was rivalry as to whose man should produce the best and make a regimental reputation. Every conceivable subject on the line of march was made to contribute to this harmless amusement and the officers encouraged it, submitting good-humoredly to being sometimes the victims themselves. The clatter of tongues and merry laughter along a dusty road would make one think they belonged to the weaker sex, bless their dear talkative hearts.[2]

Post-Civil War humor about the war was many-faced and many-toned. Certain general characteristics, however, emerge from the potpourri. Throughout the era 1865–1914 the Civil War was second only to the Negro as subject for Southern humor. Newspaper and magazine columns were filled with the humor of the war. Novels, sketches, memoirs, and short stories frequently used war themes. Unlike that written during the war, this later humor was likely to be more conciliatory than condemnatory and defiant. It was a humor that pointed with pride to the gallantry of the South's fight for independence, but it also admitted the postwar need to convert the swords into plowshares. Although not generally as realistic as the earlier humor of the Longstreet school or that written during the war, it was as consistently realistic as any humor of the postwar period. Realism bordering on naturalism is especially prominent in the memoirs of men like Sam Watkins and Carlton McCarthy who had served in the ranks. Pathos and religious sentiment were other elements of war humor often juxtaposed with vestiges of the coarse humor of before the war.

The slave was usually pictured as the Faithful Darky, who accompanied his master to war or stayed at home to tend the plantation and protect "Ol' Mistis" from the Yankees and unruly free Negroes. He would have no truck with the Yankee invaders who were trying to take him away from his rightful owners. Some slaves, like Harry S. Edwards's Isam, intervened in the war itself but failed ludicrously to become good soldiers. Others, like Harris's Uncle Remus, supported the Cause on the home front.

Although the poor white living in the mountainous areas of the South was likely to be Union in sentiment, the majority of Southern poor whites supported the Confederacy. They fought valiantly under slaveowners to protect a regime in which they had little vested interest. In humor they were typically depicted as good and brave but not very responsible or reliable soldiers. The poor-white deserter, in fact, became a familiar type in post-Civil War Southern humor.

The War for Southern Independence was the American Iliad—full of tragedy, heroism, pathos, sacrifice, hatred, and humor. Some postwar Southern humorists pointed up a defiant pride. Thomas Nelson Page, for example, in *The Burial of the Guns* (New York, 1894), had a Confederate sergeant write a note which reads: "We aint surrendered; just disbanded, and we pledges ourselves to teach our children to love the South and General Lee; and to come when we're called anywheres an' anytime, so help us God" (41). But a much more realistic and representative attitude was taken by Sam Watkins. Relating a cockfight in Atlanta in which the rooster named Southern Confederacy (Fed for short) was killed, he allegorized:

> He was a dead rooster; yea, a dead cock in the pit. Tom went and picked up his rooster, and said, "Poor Fed, I loved you; you used to crow every morning at daylight to wake me up. I have carried you a long time, but, alas! poor Fed, your days are numbered, and those who fight will sometimes be slain. Now, friends, conscripts, countrymen, if you have any tears to shed, prepare to shed them now. I will not bury Fed. The evil that roosters do lives after them, but the good is often interred with their bones. So let it be with Confed. Confed left no will, but I will pick him, and fry him, and dip my biscuit in his gravy. Poor Fed, Confed, Confederacy, I place one hand on my heart and one on my head, regretting that I have not another to place on my stomach, and whisper, softly whisper, in the most doleful accents, Good-bye, farewell, a long farewell.[3]

Most writers acknowledged that, like the namesake rooster, the Confederacy was dead beyond resurrection. The task for the living generation was, as General Lee urged, to make the South a better section within the Union. The humorists set about their work.

Notes

1. *Library of Southern Literature*, X, 4276.
2. *War Years*, 146.
3. *Co. Aytch,* 188–89.

About the Author

Wade Hall holds degrees from Troy University, the University of Alabama, and the University of Illinois. He has taught at all three universities, as well as at the University of Florida, Kentucky Southern College, and for thirty-five years at Bellarmine University, where he chaired the English, humanities, and arts programs. He is the author of numerous articles and reviews and more than twenty books about Kentucky, Alabama, and the South, including *Conecuh People: Words of Life from the Alabama Black Belt*, *An Interview with Abraham Lincoln: April 1, 1865*, and *The Outrageous Times of Larry Bruce Mitchell*, published by NewSouth Books. He now lives in his boyhood home near Union Springs, Alabama.

www.ingramcontent.com/pod-product-compliance
Lightning Source LLC
Chambersburg PA
CBHW031317060726
47590CB00003B/1251
9781603063920